TILT?

TILT?

The Search for Media Bias

DAVID NIVEN

PRAEGER

Westport, Connecticut
London

Library of Congress Cataloging-in-Publication Data

Niven, David, 1971–
    Tilt? : the search for media bias / David Niven.
        p.   cm.
    Includes bibliographical references and index.
    ISBN 0–275–97577–0 (alk. paper)
    1. Journalism—Objectivity—United States.   2. Mass media—Objectivity—United
States.   I. Title: Search for media bias.   II. Title.
    PN4888.O25N58   2002
    071'.3—dc21   2002022434

British Library Cataloguing in Publication Data is available.

Library of Congress Catalog Card Number: 2002022434
ISBN: 0–275–97577–0

First published in 2002

Praeger Publishers, 88 Post Road West, Westport, CT 06881
An imprint of Greenwood Publishing Group, Inc.
www.praeger.com

Printed in the United States of America

The paper used in this book complies with the
Permanent Paper Standard issued by the National
Information Standards Organization (Z39.48–1984).

10 9 8 7 6 5 4 3 2

Copyright Acknowledgments

Extracts from Risen, James, "Voters Reluctant to Credit Clinton for Recovery," *Los Angeles Times*, October 24, 1994 are reprinted with permission.

Extracts from Kessler, Glenn and Karen Rothmyer, "Can any of These Guys Fix the Economy?" *Newsday*, October 11, 1992 are reprinted with permission.

Contents

Illustrations

FIGURES

Preface

Nurses. Pharmacists. Veterinarians. Doctors. School teachers. Clergy. Professors. Dentists. Engineers. Policemen. Judges. Accountants. Bankers. Funeral directors. Governors. Local officeholders. U.S. Senators. Building contractors. Business executives. Auto mechanics. U.S. Representatives. State officeholders. Stockbrokers. Labor union leaders. Lawyers. Real estate agents.

When the Gallup Poll asked Americans to rate the honesty and ethics of people in various fields, all of these occupations were more trusted than "newspaper reporters."[1] Americans ranked the honesty and ethics of newspaper reporters ahead of only car salesmen, insurance salesmen, and the advertising industry. In numbers like these, it is clear to observers such as *New York Times* columnist Frank Rich that "everyone hates the media."[2]

At the foundation of this problem is distrust and a belief that the media are biased. Alarmingly, almost nine in ten Americans believe members of the media are regularly influenced by their personal views when covering politics.[3]

The problem is so obvious, according to columnist Charles Krauthammer, writing in *Newsday*, "That it would take a mollusk to miss the pattern."[4] The exact pattern in question, according to Krauthammer, countless other critics, and much of the American populace, is the media's liberal bias.

Charges of bias fly, and sociologist Herbert Gans, for one, worries that "journalists are condemned as a new class of villains whose values threaten America" (1985, 29). Communications scholar Everette Dennis notes, "It is almost impossible to open a newspaper or turn on the car radio these days and not hear a denunciation of the 'liberal news media' and what Rush Limbaugh and others call 'their latest outrages'" (1997, 115).

While we have seen a groundswell of support for the notion that the media are biased, little research has subjected these beliefs to meaningful tests. Much like Justice Potter Stewart's definition of pornography, we "know" the media are biased because we see it that way. But are the media really biased? Would an objective comparison of coverage produce evidence of bias? Much research has been done, but much of it lacks any kind of fair baseline on which to judge coverage. Nevertheless, the charges pervade discussions of the media.

THE "COMMUNIST, PINKO" MEDIA

As dependably as the swallows return to Capistrano, Republican presidential candidates return to very familiar territory in decrying the "biased liberal media." Indeed, almost all of the potential Republican contenders in the 2000 race voiced concerns about media bias.

Republican hopeful Steve Forbes, in a 1999 fundraising letter, wrote that the battle against liberals ("whose deviousness and malice have passed all civilized standards") must begin with the "liberal media." According to Forbes, it is the liberal media that saved President Bill Clinton from having to resign in disgrace.[5] Not to be outdone, Senator John McCain eloquently expressed his objection to the liberal media in his reference to NBC network news anchor Tom Brokaw as a "Trotskyite ... left wing, Communist, pinko."[6]

Moreover, Republican presidents, vice presidents, and nominees dating back at least to the Eisenhower administration have complained about media bias. 1996 Republican nominee Bob Dole blamed the liberal media for its prominent coverage of his statement that tobacco was not addictive, as well as other mistreatments.[7] Dole's dismay over the liberal media had actually simmered for over two decades. Memorably, Dole proclaimed in 1972 that "the greatest political scandal of this campaign is the brazen manner in which, without benefit of clergy, the *Washington*

Post has set up housekeeping with the McGovern campaign" (Quoted in Bernstein and Woodward 1974, 182).

Both Presidents George H.W. Bush and George W. Bush took umbrage with a liberal media that George W. saw as "trying to hurt" the Bushes "through unbelievable allegations."[8] The first President Bush took delight at his 1992 campaign appearances in waving a bumper sticker that read, "Annoy the Media, Re-Elect George Bush."

As the 2000 presidential race heated up, Republicans took an even more forward approach to their grievances. Jim Nicholson, Republican National Committee chair, distributed the phone numbers of network news anchors Brokaw, Peter Jennings, and Dan Rather to Republican activists across the country in protest over media bias toward Democrats.[9]

OVERVIEW

This research will explore the scope and effect of media bias charges and put these allegations to the test. *Tilt?* explores how allegations of media bias are covered (chapter 1), the state of public opinion on the media (chapter 2), and the previous conclusions of academic researchers about media fairness (chapter 3). Then, in chapter 4, *Tilt?* turns to a unique and fair method for measuring bias in the media in a comparison of coverage of Democratic and Republican office holders. In chapter 5, evidence for other potential forms of media bias is explored. Chapter 6 offers a summary of the findings, an exploration of the effects of our propensity to cry "bias," and a prescription for improving our perception of the media.

NOTES

1. Gallup Honesty and Ethics in Professions Report, November 2000 (www.gallup.com/poll/findings/indhnsty_ethcs2asp).

2. *New York Times*, January 29, 2000.

3. October 2000 poll by the Pew Research Center for the People and the Press (www.people-press.org). See chapter 2 for more information.

4. Krauthammer, Charles. 2000. "Does the Media Lean Leftward? It Certainly Does." *Newsday*, October 4.

5. *Washington Post*, January 3, 1999.

6. *New York Times*, February 2, 2000.
7. *San Diego Union-Tribune*, July 6, 1996.
8. *New York Times*, August 18, 1992.
9. *Palm Beach Post*, March 7, 2000.

Acknowledgments

This work has taken shape in my teaching of a Media and Politics course at Florida Atlantic University. Many of my students there participated in this exploration of media bias through various class projects and independent study projects. I appreciate their efforts and their interest, without which the comparisons of media coverage presented here would not have been possible.

My interest in this topic was first sparked in a Political Behavior seminar at Ohio State University taught by Herb Asher. In a momentary digression apropos of nothing, Herb asserted that no one had ever done an adequate job testing for the existence of media bias. He looked around the room and challenged us to offer a better way to measure media bias. While it is years too late to submit this as my term paper, I hope it will suffice.

Some of the results presented in chapters 4 and 5 were previously published in articles that appeared in *Social Science Quarterly* and the *Harvard International Journal of Press/Politics*.

This research was supported by grants from the American Political Science Association and the Shorenstein Center, Kennedy School of Government, Harvard University.

CHAPTER 1

Slanted Headlines: How the Media Cover Media Bias

Perhaps nowhere in society is an entity entrusted with as much responsibility, while at the same time being subject to such widespread distrust, as the media.[1] While we Americans continually depend on conventional media outlets for information regarding politics and government (see, for example, Althaus and Tewksbury 2000; Dalton, Beck, and Huckfeldt 1998; Eveland and Scheufele 2000; Kwak 1999; Lowden, Andersen, and Dozier 1994), we simultaneously believe the processes and participants that bring us the news are so inherently flawed that they can only be regarded as biased (Gaziano 1988; Gaziano and McGrath 1986; Gunther 1988; Gunther 1992; Lipset and Schneider 1987; Rimmer and Weaver 1987; Watts, Domke, Shah, and Fan 1999).

One of the interesting aspects of the debate over media bias is that, unlike other institutions that might face criticism, the media are both the subjects of criticism and the vessels by which that criticism is spread. Tire makers accused of manufacturing bad tires do not decide how much we should hear about the problem, or which speakers should be allowed to describe it. Politicians embroiled in a scandal cannot dictate the terms under which their indiscretions are detailed to the American people. The media, on the other hand, are expected not only to be the watchdog of other people and organizations, but also the watchdog of themselves.

While there are obviously alternative means of delivering a

message including Internet web sites and discussion groups dedicated to criticizing the media, the most widely disseminated source of information about media bias is still the conventional media. The potential importance of how that media portray their own capacity for fairness is great. Such coverage may be affecting how we perceive the media, how we react to its information, and ultimately how we perceive our government. Nevertheless, there have been few studies dedicated to exploring how the media cover media bias.

One work on this topic, by Mark Watts, David Domke, Dhavan Shah, and David Fan (1999), reaches the intriguing conclusion that a bigger factor in understanding perceptions of media bias than the actual fairness of media coverage is the quantity of coverage on bias. They compare coverage of presidential candidates over multiple elections and find that the balance of coverage between the Democratic and Republican nominee has little influence on public assessments of media bias. Conversely, public perceptions of bias have grown with "increasing news self-coverage . . . on the general topic of bias" (144). Moreover, this coverage of bias is unrelated to the presence of bias (159). Which is to say, coverage of bias does not rise or fall in proportion to the media's treatment of Republicans and Democrats.

Watts and colleagues do find that media coverage of media bias is overwhelmingly directed toward allegations of pro-liberal/pro-Democratic bias. Indeed, suggestions of liberal media bias outnumber claims of conservative bias by a margin of four to one (159). The ubiquity of liberal media charges coupled with the tendency to indict not just a single reporter or news outlet, but rather the entire media industry, suggest that the media are projecting an "hegemonic frame" of liberal bias to the American people (159).

The significance of this coverage pattern is magnified by the difficulty of accurately assessing the evidence. Watts's team argues that people are ill-equipped to counter charges of media bias with anything approaching reality: "The political environment seems much too complex for people to keep a running tally of whether media coverage is fair or unfair to a candidate or party" (167). Thus, the messages elites send us can have tremendous influence over our opinions on such unwieldy subjects (See, for example, Jasperson, Shah, Watts, Faber, and Fan (1998).

While their study does not focus on the origin of this pattern in coverage, Watts and his coauthors suggest the disarming possibility that some portion of the coverage of the media's liberal bias is a defense mechanism. In other words, failing to adequately cover charges of media bias could be viewed as just another example of media bias, leading to even more charges of bias (Watts, Domke, Shah, and Fan 1999, 168).

A YEAR IN THE LIFE OF MEDIA BIAS

To explore the nature of media bias coverage and to expand on the available research, this chapter provides a content analysis of media coverage of media bias during the period of September 1, 2000 to August 31, 2001.

Articles on media bias were located in the Lexis-Nexis "major newspaper" database, which includes approximately sixty of the largest newspapers in the United States.[2] Articles were included in the analysis if they used a bias phrase (media bias, liberal bias, conservative bias, Democratic bias, Republican bias) and that bias reference pertained to the media (newspapers, television, or radio). Overall, the database yielded 632 articles that referred to media bias. Each of the articles was read by a member of a team of student coders participating in a class project. The articles were analyzed for their perspective (what kind of bias was alleged), their tone (was the article entirely one-sided, or were differing opinions included?), the form of bias alleged (what was the type of evidence for bias?) and finally to whom the source of bias information was attributed. Table 1.1 summarizes the findings.

THE BIAS PERSPECTIVE

To determine the perspective of the article, coders analyzed the headline and lead paragraph, and then counted the number of paragraphs in the full text of the article that offered information on bias. If two of those three (or three of three) indicators were in agreement, the article was coded in that direction. In other words, if the headline and most of the paragraphs suggested the media had a liberal bias, then the article was coded "liberal." If two of the three suggested a conservative bias, then the article was coded "conservative." If two of three indicators suggested the media were fair, then the article was coded "no bias."[3]

Perhaps the most important pattern in the results appears in line one of Table 1.1. Of the 632 articles that discuss media bias,

Table 1.1
Newspaper Coverage of Media Bias, 2000–2001

	Conservative Bias/Republican Bias	Liberal Bias/Democratic Bias	No Bias
Proportion of all articles	81	5	14
Tone (% mention opposing opinion)	35	95	100
Form of Bias			
Unequal Treatment	70	65	n/a
Unrealistic/ Incomplete	65	57	n/a
Mean/Sarcastic/ Unflattering	62	29	n/a
Labeling	27	10	n/a
Issues	58	42	n/a
Sources			
Politicians	40	6	5
Academics	15	52	60
Interest Groups	40	32	10
''Fair Sounding'' Groups	25	10	0
Media	48	57	90
People	38	1	0

N = 632

Source: Analysis of articles from the Lexis-Nexis "Major Newspapers" index, September 1, 2000–August 31, 2001.

an overwhelming 81 percent purport to substantiate allegations of a pro-liberal/Democratic, anti-conservative/Republican bias. The claim that the media are unbiased predominates in 14 percent of the articles, while only 5 percent of the articles assert there is a pro-conservative/Republican, anti-liberal/Democratic bias in the media. Thus, according to these figures, the American news consumer gets sixteen times as many messages that the media have a liberal bias as it does that the media have a conservative bias, and six times as many messages that the media are biased as it does that the media are fair.

Further ammunition for claims of liberal bias is also provided in the way articles on bias were presented. Coders read each article to see if any voice was allowed to offer the opposite conclusion. In other words, in an article that largely points to liberal bias, was there a source in the article who disagreed with the assertion and was given space to explain that disagreement? (Some articles mentioned those who disagreed with the article's conclusion only to mock their close-mindedness. Those articles were coded as not having provided an opposition response.)

Overall, the contrast between liberal bias articles and the other two categories is huge. In only 35 percent of liberal bias stories is there any space dedicated to the arguments of someone who disagrees with the conclusion of liberal media bias. That compares with the 95 percent of conservative bias stories that included opposition thoughts, and the 100 percent of no bias stories that included assertions that contradict the article's position.

Thus, not only are there more stories that allege liberal bias, those stories are more likely to present the situation in absolute terms. The far fewer articles that come to different conclusions, meanwhile, almost unanimously acknowledge those with conflicting opinions.

While this difference in coverage and tone of coverage is vast, the implications for reinforcement are even greater. Media studies sometimes question the ability of the media to change our opinions or actions, but there is widespread agreement that, with the selective attention of the consumer, the media can serve to bolster beliefs we already have (for example, Meffert 2000). For example, when countless Americans open the newspaper in the morning with a preexisting skepticism about their information provider, they are prone to believe any news evidence that supports their skepticism. They then find articles in which the newspaper itself calls into question the fairness of its own product or of its industry in general. In the process, a powerful, self-indicting message is communicated to a largely receptive audience.

INDICATORS OF BIAS

The articles were also scrutinized for the evidence cited as indicating bias. Based on results from a small sample of articles, categories of evidence were created that included unequal treatment, unrealistic/incomplete treatment, mean/sarcastic/unflattering treatment, use of labels, and negative coverage of issues.

Articles could include multiple indicators of bias. Thus, the results in the Form of Bias section of Table 1.1 do not total 100. For obvious reasons, the evidence of bias indicator does not include the articles that conclude the media are unbiased.

Bias was alleged in matters large and small. Newspapers received complaints from readers, writers, and participants in politics on everything from the placement of stories, the lengths of stories, the use or failure to use extended quotes from a speaker, and whether the party and ideology of political actors was consistently applied.[4]

Most frequently, in both liberal bias and conservative bias stories, bias was alleged in situations in which a member of one party was treated differently than the member of another. Why, for example, did a Democratic Senator get more publicity for his dairy bill than a Republican representative did for the same piece of legislation, a *Star-Tribune* reader asked the paper.[5] Why are some candidates allowed to get away with absurd overstatements when others are called to task for minor misstatements, another commentator wondered with regard to the media as a whole.[6] And in the case of Bryant Gumbel, presumably the question asked is, Why has he been caught muttering (after he had finished the segment and thrown the cameras to the weather report, but alas, before the microphone had been turned off) "What a f——— idiot" after finishing an interview with a conservative activist, but never with a liberal guest.[7]

Given the year under study, it is probably not surprising that a great number of articles on bias in general and on unequal treatment in particular referred to the presidential race. Al Gore was said to be the beneficiary of a media bias that did everything from declaring him the winner early on election night [8] to making sure that George W. Bush was the butt of more jokes on late night television.[9] Charles Krauthhammer, writing in *Newsday*, claimed that from day one the Gore agenda had been openly favored by the media. He noted what he considered to be one of the most egregious examples in a *New York Times* headline (September 7, 2000) "Gore Offers Vision of Better Times For Middle Class." Krauthhammer called it "the kind of headline Pravda used to run for Leonid Brezhnev's campaigns."[10]

In the months after the election, many articles suggested that President Bush had received unfair coverage in relation to the treatment received when Bill Clinton was elected. In a *Pittsburgh*

Post-Gazette op-ed column, Jack Kelly wrote that the difference even extended to the first family's children: "The news media rarely invaded the privacy of Chelsea Clinton. Contrast that with the media orgy that erupted when Jenna Bush tried to buy a margarita."[11]

There were also a few critics who saw unequal treatment indicators suggestive of a conservative bias in the media. The *Boston Globe* reported that "George W. Bush has had the better of it on the question of character" since journalists were "far more likely to pick up on Bush's core theme of compassionate conservatism and reform than they were to trumpet Gore's pet theme of competence and experience."[12] Meanwhile, the *New York Times'* Paul Krugman argued that "the mainstream media are fanatically determined to seem evenhanded," and in their obsession they have actually "failed to call Bush to account on even the most outrageous misstatements. . . . If [Bush] were to declare that the earth is flat, you would be sure to see a news analysis under the headline 'Shape of the Planet: Both Sides Have a Point.' After all, the earth isn't perfectly spherical."[13]

There were also those who drew a contrast between the treatment of President Bush and his predecessor, and concluded that the zest for scandal under Clinton suggests a conservative bias.[14]

To be sure, sightings of unequal treatment were not limited to the two major parties. Even the partyless governor of Minnesota, Jesse Ventura, singled out the media's interest in the bankruptcy and dissolution of the XFL sports league after having shown little interest in the league during its short existence. Governor Ventura, who had moonlighted while in office as a television analyst for the league, said of the coverage, "Tell me that's not media bias. When it folds, oh it's, 'We got a chance to get the governor. We can nail him.' "[15]

The significance of "unequal treatment" as an indicator of bias is that it offers the shine of scientific certainty. One can point to the way two candidates or two presidents were treated, seize on differences, and then on the firm foundation of those differences substantiate bias. The problem with this approach, as will be discussed in later chapters, is that few people in politics can legitimately lay a claim to equal treatment. If one candidate gets better treatment, perhaps the candidate had better ideas, ran a better campaign, or received a warmer response from the American people. Surely no two presidents can be expected to receive equal coverage given the incredible variations among the situations they face and their ultimate performance in office. Nonetheless, despite these logical caveats, coverage of "unequal treatment" in bias articles is prevalent and powerful.

For liberal media articles, the other major categories that appear most regularly are "unrealistic/incomplete treatment" and "mean/sarcastic/unflattering treatment." While both these categories are more abstract than the first, they often add incendiary language into the bias discussion. For conservative media articles, "unrealistic/incomplete treatment" and coverage of issues are the second and third most prevalent categories.

WHO CALLS THE MEDIA BIASED?

In addition to the direction of the articles and the substance of the evidence, coders were also asked to categorize the source of bias information. Coders read each article and categorized the speaker associated with making a claim of bias (or denying it) into one of six categories: (1) Politicians and ideological figures (includes elected officials, those associated with a party, and those who carry some identification as being associated with the right or left), (2) Academics (includes those who teach as well as those associated with think tanks), (3) Interest groups (includes all those associated with an advocacy group), (4) "Fair-sounding" interest groups (includes those relatively unknown groups with names that suggest they are interested solely in a fair-minded media), (5) The media (includes the voice of the author of the article and any quote attributed to a writer, reporter, or media professional), and (6) The people (includes anyone presented as a regular, unaffiliated observer). Articles could include multiple sources. Thus, the sources section of Table 1.1 does not total 100 percent.

In considering the results listed in Table 1.1, we can see that the scope and certainty of media bias is conveyed not only through the sheer number of articles, their tone, and the evidence provided, but also through the important factor of who is allowed to speak on the issue. In coverage alleging liberal media bias, the most frequent speakers are not just conservative politicos, but a vast range of sources that carry the imprimatur of objectivity (such as regular people, fair-sounding groups, etc.) as well as those who would seem to have an interest in denying bias, namely the media itself. Through the range of speakers and the passion with which they speak, a very definite message is conveyed that a consensus of diverse observers has concluded the media are biased toward liberals.

To be sure, some of those who speak out on media bias have a vested interest in making their argument. The National Rifle Association (NRA) is one group whose antipathy for the media is clear, but whose political agenda is also obvious. Nevertheless, coverage of bias based on the claims of partisan groups can be quite vivid. As the *Kansas City Star* reported, "The National Rifle Association is in battle with a biased, hypocritical and out-of-touch liberal media for the hearts and minds of Americans, according to a panel of conservative pundits at the group's convention in Kansas City. 'The NRA is regularly mocked and satirized in news coverage, with a great number of joke headlines,' said Susan Howard, an . . . NRA board member."[16]

Claims of media bias are also attributed to the likes of Jesse Helms,[17] Rush Limbaugh,[18] Republicans in general,[19] or even every conservative alive.[20] Nevertheless, it is notable how many of those who allege media bias are portrayed as non-political actors who voice concerns about media bias solely in their pursuit of objectivity.

Plain, reliable-sounding, regular people are a source of bias information in over one-third of the articles written on the liberal bias. As the former editor of the *Atlanta Journal and Constitution* put it in a homey, feel-good version of the media bias story, "old codgers" with a "lifelong interest in public affairs" and a dedication to reading newspapers "often call on me to explain liberal bias in newspapers. Over a recent midday snack, the old codgers agreed President George W. Bush has received the worst, and most biased, coverage of any president in their memory, which I might point out, goes back a long way, although not quite to Teddy Roosevelt." For many of these objective sounding, real people sources, bias is no mere allegation, it is a fact. "Newspapers didn't used to be biased the way they are now," another old codger explained to the Atlanta newspaper.[21]

In a similar vein, the *Christian Science Monitor* reported that "readers across the U.S. charged newspapers with having a liberal bias" in response to media coverage of the presidential recount and the months-long media review of the recount.[22] According to the press coverage, not only does the average American see media bias,[23] even teenagers understand the media are unfair.[24]

While average people are finding bias, distinguished and fair sounding groups are also on the case. The Media Research Center put out a list of "the most biased, manipulative or downright goofy quotes uttered by liberals in the 'mainstream' news media."[25] There was no mention of who or what the Media Research Center is, or that it is comprised solely of extreme conservatives. The Statistical Assessment Service, meanwhile, outlined its findings on press coverage of stem cell research and concluded that "media bias plays an important role in the information that is being published on the subject," and that coverage favors such research.[26] Again, there is no mention of the makeup of this group, which—although a distinctly conservative organization—sounds utterly scientific.

Individual "experts" can receive similar treatment. *Newsday* called the same analyst, Charles Cook, as "fair-minded and well-regarded an analyst" as one could hope to find,[27] and the *Washington Post* called him as "nonpartisan an observer" as one could hope to find.[28] Given Cook's impressive objectivity, when he declared that reporters were " 'larding their stories with their own ideological biases' in favor of Gore"[29] and that "it was not a pretty sight,"[30] the pronouncement was covered as a scientific certainty. What was missing from this picture is the fact that in addition to being a political analyst, Cook's political preferences are in the conservative direction.

The distinction here is significant. Bias claims from those in politics may be discounted because of the self-serving nature of the complaints. But bias claims from "regular people," buttressed by bias claims from noted and fair experts, begin to seem not only legitimate, but difficult to dispute. Another major voice asserting liberal bias makes the conclusion all the more ironclad, because many in the media are saying it about themselves.

Much of the media's self-criticism is found in the words of columnists. For syndicated writer George Will, Al Gore's loss in the election of 2000 is astounding when you consider "he ran with gale-force economic winds at his back, and with a powerful media bias pulling him along."[31] *Boston Herald* columnist Howie Carr decried coverage of the presidential recount with, "I have a few questions about the coverage of the media's monthlong telethon for the man who invented the Internet."[32] Jack Kelly, writing in the *Pittsburgh Post Gazette* asserts that "the 'mainstream' media have gone well beyond merely the appearance of impropriety."[33]

Notice the quotes around mainstream, to further accentuate their position, presumably as social outcasts. *Rocky Mountain News* columnist Mike Rosen summed up the conclusions of many writers when he said of media bias in 2000, "The only change this year is that they were even more blatant about it."[34] Robert Samuelson even argues that one manifestation of the media's bias toward liberals is the media's unwillingness to admit their bias. "Among editors and reporters of the national media—papers, magazines, TV—a 'liberal bias' is not so much denied as ignored, despite overwhelming evidence that it exists."[35]

And it doesn't stop there. According to the media coverage, the pro-liberal, pro-Democratic bias that pervades the "seven sisters of the liberal media (CBS, NBC, ABC, the *New York Times*, the *Washington Post*, *Time*, and *Newsweek*)"[36] has also taken hold in entertainment programming. Evidence includes the liberal preferences of the main characters on the *West Wing*.[37]

In some cases the media are not just biased, but biased and ignorant, as syndicated columnist (and, briefly, Bush administration nominee for secretary of labor) Linda Chavez asserts: "Media bias doesn't stem solely from the fact that most of the press corps vote Democrat (a phenomenon that goes back at least 20 years). The problem is more complicated. The reporters who cover politics are generally not experts on policy. And few reporters, including those whose expertise stretches beyond politics, have even a modest understanding of how the U.S. economy works."[38]

Media bias is so obvious to many writers that it requires neither an explanation nor any facts. As one report on a Republican activists' forum put it, "Save for a few pesky obstacles—their rejection by minorities, the liberal bias of the media and California's steadfast determination to elect Democrats—conservatives are in seventh heaven."[39] In other words, in a news article meant to presents only facts in the voice of the writer, the statistical certainty of minorities' preference for the Democratic Party, and the party's recent sweep of California Senate seats, the governor's office, and the state's electoral college vote, is paralleled by the undeniable bias of the media against conservatives and Republicans.

Even in situations in which many would assume negative coverage of a Republican is fully warranted, some in the media turn right back to bias. Mike Rosen on George W. Bush's campaign misadventure with an open microphone: "George W. was inadvertently caught referring to *New York Times* reporter Adam Clymer as an 'a———.' It's a shame so much of the coverage of this story has dwelled on the epithet itself, rather than the substance of the charge. . . . What Bush meant was that this Clymer guy is one of those liberal media types who write editorials masquerading as news stories knocking Republicans and praising Democrats."[40]

Indeed, Bush's presidency has been attacked, according to Michael Kelly, writing in the *Dayton Daily News*, "because most reporters do not approve of his policies. Because they are conservative policies. This is the bias that endures."[41]

According to their own colleagues, not only are the media guilty of liberal bias, they are likely to fall back on whines and complaints rather than evidence in defending their trade. As Charles Krauthammer put, "When the subject of liberal bias in the media is brought up, particularly during an election campaign, journalists tend to roll their eyes and groan 'there you go again' at this recrudescence of an old right-wing shibboleth."[42]

Importantly, it is not just those who are paid to express opinions, and who tend to do so from the right side of the political spectrum, who give voice to allegations of media bias. Many on the ostensibly objective side of the news business also decry media bias. Former ABC White House correspondent and current Fox News Channel anchor and managing editor Brit Hume is one of many outspoken voices in the media on the subject of the media. Hume says, "The media are not disposed toward Republican presidents—any Republican president—and really never have been."[43] Hume adds, "It's hard to find an anti-abortion reporter in Washington. It's hard to find a reporter not worried about environmental protection. It's hard to find a reporter who doesn't view tax cuts as an attempt to help the rich at the expense of everybody else. Joe Lieberman's religion is a point in his favor. John Ashcroft's religious convictions are being used by a lot of people to oppose him. That's just the way it is."[44]

Even when the objective writer is not personally voicing complaints about media bias, in their choice of subjects they are frequently advancing the belief. The *Washington Post*'s media columnist Howard Kurtz, for example, has given a forum to many of the leading anti-media voices, including the aforementioned Mike Rosen, who was quoted by Kurtz as saying of the media coverage of Campaign 2000, "In their souls [the media] desperately don't want the Republicans to control Congress and a Republican president, to name the next two or three Supreme Court justices. This is the most egregiously spun campaign that I've seen."[45] In the same article, Kurtz quoted another conservative commentator as saying that journalists are "little more than a spin machine for the Democratic Party" and that "journalists themselves have concluded that the mainstream media are tilting heavily toward Vice President Gore." As for rebuttal, Kurtz offered this tepid rejoinder, "Most journalists dismiss such charges of liberal bias as a stale stereotype.[46]

Surveys

Another source of liberal/Democratic bias evidence is the use of surveys. Survey results of reporters, presented with the associated air of scientific certainly, consistently indicate that more reporters are liberal/Democratic than conservative/Republican, and that the proportion of reporters supporting the left exceeds the proportion in the general population.

Columnist Robert Samuelson, writing in the *San Diego Union-Tribune*, noted that a Kaiser Foundation poll showed that reporters were only one-sixth as likely to be conservatives in comparison to the U.S. population as a whole. Samuelson calls this "overwhelming evidence" of liberal media bias.[47] Charles Krauthhammer, in the same article in which he compared the U.S. media to Pravda, noted that a Roper poll of reporters "found that in 1992 they had voted 89 percent for Clinton, 7 percent for Bush. Regular Americans had voted Clinton over Bush, 43 percent to 38 percent. The country went marginally for Clinton; the journalists went for him 13 to 1. In other words, for every seven Bush voters among the American people, there were eight Clinton voters. But for every seven Bush voters in the Washington media, there were 89 for Clinton. Margins of victory that lopsided are rarely seen this side of Syria."[48]

In striking contrast to articles linking our media to the Soviets and Syrians, when a survey of television news producers found that more were voting for Bush than Gore, there was little coverage of the finding and even less outrage. The *Rocky Mountain News*, one of the few outlets to cover the story, labeled the finding that Bush trumped Gore among a media group only "a bit surprising."[49]

In addition to surveys of media professionals, surveys of readers are also used to illustrate the prevalence of bias. The *Christian Science Monitor* reported just before the 2000 election that voters who thought the media were unfair to George W. Bush outnumbered those who thought the media were unfair to Al Gore by a margin of two to one.[50] Similarly, a *Boston Globe* article in October 2000 reported that two thirds of voters thought that "most journalists were rooting for Gore."[51]

Taken together, the sources who speak for liberal bias offer the appearance of certainty, credibility, common sense, and even at times, scientific proof. This is a case made not only by apparently interested parties (though they are heard from), and not only by interest groups with a clear agenda (though they are present as well), but a case made by experts and regular people alike, and importantly, one made regularly by the media itself. Indeed, research in other fields shows there is nothing as damning in deciding guilt as a confession (for example, Kassin 1997).

WHO DENIES THE MEDIA ARE BIASED?

The contrast between those who advance the notion that the media are biased toward liberals and those who disagree is substantial. While the media bias case is made by a well-rounded group of political actors, nonpartisan experts, regular people, and the media itself, the case against media bias is largely left to be made by academics and reporters. Importantly, the media retain a far greater credibility when they are pointing out their faults than when they are defending themselves. Moreover, the academic voices who join in the media's defense are apt to be written off as having the same biases as the media themselves.

Academics

Scan the articles that suggest the media are not biased against conservatives and Republicans and you will see professors given a prominent position. A New York University professor chalks up claims of media bias to "paranoia in the Republican Party."[52] A researcher at Harvard University is quoted as saying the CBS Evening News "should be applauded,"[53] not called biased, for its decision not to cover the scandal surrounding Democratic Representative Gary Condit. A retired professor from the University of Pennsylvania notes that "No networks or big newspapers are owned by the AFL-CIO, Friends of the Earth or the Socialist Workers Party. . . . The media are owned by big for-profit corporations [and] rely for the majority of their revenue on advertisers, who are mostly other corporations that want their ads to appear in a supportive selling environment."[54]

Even when the thrust of an academic's comments claim is that the media are not biased against conservatives, his or her words can sometimes be used to give the opposite impression.[55] For example, in an article quoting a professor's finding that there is no media bias against Republicans, the headline reads, "The bad news is, there's bias everywhere."[56]

While academics are the main source outside of the media that denies bias, they are generally quoted without the context of research findings. In the process, they can appear to be little more than cheerleaders for the media. Moreover, the complete absence of "regular people" defending the media only serves to underscore the basic argument that the media are an elitist group of liberals, connected to academics, another elitist group of liberals, and totally disconnected from regular people.

Mike King, writing in response to reader concerns about bias at the *Atlanta Journal and Constitution*, worries about how far reporters are from normal people, a situation he thinks inevitably leads to bias. "Perhaps if more of us were PTA members, or worked on community-service projects, or reached out to spend time away from the job with people who don't look like us, weren't raised like us, didn't get the advantages we take for granted—maybe then we would connect more with the people we claim to be serving," King argues. "And maybe they'd come to believe we can be fair."[57]

The Media Defense

While members of the media are often in the forefront of the attack against their own industry, many in the media are wont to speak in their defense regarding charges of bias. There are two major distinctions between the media's self-defense and those in the media who charge media bias. First, a defense is far less credible since many assume it to be motivated by self-interest (regardless of the self-interest that may motivate those in the media who attack the media).[58] Second, the tone and nature of the media defenders is quite different from the media attackers. We previously saw that these articles are almost three times as likely to give some room to those who disagree with the main premise of the writer. Moreover, the voices of defenders do not berate and shout.

In many depictions, defenders of the media seem to lack debating skills or lack interest as they simply "insist there was no media bias."[59] Defenders do not point fingers and root out corruption, instead they almost express amusement with the topic. Lesley Stahl, a reporter on CBS' *60 Minutes*, flippantly proclaimed that there was no media bias, and that she operated without bias because, "I had my opinions surgically removed when I became a network correspondent."[60]

Many media commentaries defending against charges of bias are in the form of newspaper editors' responses to reader complaints. Here the comments tend to strike a note of conciliation and—even while denying bias—have a tendency to acknowledge some of the main premises of those with whom they disagree. Comments from John Craig, the editor of the *Pittsburgh Post-Gazette*, were typical. Craig makes the case that while the paper's staff strive to be comprehensive and fair, "being stimulating and provocative are also a vital part of the equation." Avoiding bias is a worthy goal, but hewing too closely to that objective will leave you with a boring product, and "no editor wants his paper to be hated, but that is better than not being read at all." Craig writes of a higher goal than being popular on every issue. "There is no doubt that in many cases the majority of readers do not agree with the newspaper's position—consider only the matter of editorial endorsements. That is good, not bad. I say that not because of arrogance or insensitivity, but out of a conviction that a reputation for honesty and dependability is the best bet in the long run, unpopular though it may be at times."[61]

Craig, like many others who provide official media responses to charges of bias, does not so much deny them as make a case for understanding them. Similarly, the *Atlanta Journal and Constitution*'s ombudsperson, Mike King, focuses not on disputing the potential for media bias within his organization, but on establishing the wall of separation between (the presumably biased) editorial board and (the presumably fair) reporters. King explains, "Readers are convinced, for instance, that Cythnia Tucker and the editorial writers of the *Constitution* share their opinions with news editors and reporters, influencing what we cover and how we cover it. In fact, the two groups rarely meet, and for the most part reporters at the newspaper read the editorial opinions of the paper the same time you do—after they are printed. Suffice it to say that the wall between the newsroom and the opinion writers at the newspaper actually does exist."[62] However, even if King proves to readers this wall exists, that does not preclude the personal preferences of the reporters from influencing coverage.

Joanne Ostrow, writing in the *Denver Post*, simultaneously denies media bias, but acknowledges the main claim of those who believe in it. "Whenever anyone complains about a perceived 'liberal media bias,' they ought to note that the folks in the trenches, the working stiffs carrying the notepads, cameras and microphones, may tend toward the left. But the people signing the paychecks, buying and selling stations, negotiating mergers, running the shareholder meetings and lobbying Congress are clearly on the right."[63]

Michael Kinsley, in a *Washington Post* op-ed article, humorously denied the existence of bias, but likely fueled belief in so doing. Kinsley described a poll he conducted among the staffers of the on-line magazine *Slate*, of which Kinsley is the editor. Kinsley found that the vast majority of his staffers supported Al Gore over George W. Bush. While admitting this reality, Kinsley laments that "fear of confirming conservative suspicions about the liberal predisposition of the media is probably the main reason other journalists will resist following our lead" in polling their staffs and recognizing their liberal/Democratic preferences.

With all that on the table, Kinsley then makes the case for why such results do not matter. "This is a natural result of the sort of people who are attracted to various careers. It is not the product of any conspiracy. There is no Liberal Central Committee drafting young liberals into journalism against their will, or blackballing young conservatives," Kinsley wrote. Further, "there is nothing that can be done to change this disparity, unless conservative press critics would like to see the media institute a political quota system, favoring conservatives over better-qualified liberals (affirmative action for opponents of affirmative action)."[64]

Others dispute charges of media bias by making the claim that the problem with the media is not the political bias, but the titillation bias. Chris Thomas, in the *Arizona Republic*, wrote, "A media with a liberal bias would not have carpet-bombed us with coverage of Monica Lewinsky, Hillary Clinton's fishy commodities deal, the president's fund-raising, and the deaths of Clintonites

Vince Foster and Ron Brown. . . . So long as there's something entertaining to push, it matters little to the media what it is. Like processed 'cheese food,' political issues are homogenized and pressed into the same easy-to-swallow news product. There isn't any media conspiracy to run political news through a liberal filter. There isn't any conservative filter. There isn't any filter at all."[65]

Few and far between are the articles that claim that there is a media bias in the opposite direction, that is, against liberals and for conservatives. As is the case for the articles asserting no bias, again the main voices here are academics and the media itself.

Interestingly, much of the coverage that makes this assertion theorizes that the media have been bullied by media bias accusations into treating Republicans better. As Robert Scheer of the *Los Angeles Times* put it, "Intimidated by the right wing's absurd claim of a liberal bias, journalists tend to be hard on Democrats while granting Republicans a free pass."[66] Similarly, the *Baltimore Sun's* Tom Teepen wrote that "perhaps gun shy after years of conservative accusations of liberal bias, the press gave Mr. Bush a bye and Mr. Gore a going-over."[67]

A few articles noted the research conclusions of groups studying the coverage of the 2000 presidential race as well as the endorsements in that race. Both methods yielded the finding that Bush was the recipient of more positive coverage, coverage that more frequently communicated his core message, and received the majority of newspaper endorsements.[68] But these findings were buried under a mountain of articles asserting the opposite.

Nonetheless, inherent in the act of defending against charges is vulnerability. In fact, criminal justice studies find that the more information provided in denying a charge, the less credible a person is judged to be (for example, Holtgraves and Grayer 1994). Those who deny that the media are biased toward liberals are not just outnumbered, they are undercut by their very positions. The case for liberal bias, then, is made not only in the amount of coverage, the tone of that coverage, the evidence provided, and in the apparently fair-minded comprehensive sources that know the media are biased, but also in the very dynamic of making a charge versus mounting a defense.

The Fight: Critic versus Media

At times, the charges and responses in the media bias discussion get far more pointed and specific between a politician and a newspaper. It is an interesting dynamic, as a critic launches an attack on a media outlet armed with an array of barbs but is dependent on media outlets to share those criticisms if they are to be heard.

Senator Mitch McConnell of Kentucky, running for reelection in 2000, nevertheless took on the state's largest newspaper, The *Courier-Journal* of Louisville. McConnell, a conservative Republican, claimed the paper was attempting to hurt not only his political standing, but also that of his wife, Kentucky Secretary of Labor Elaine L. Chao.[69]

As the *New York Times* reported, McConnell counted nineteen "attack articles, editorials and cartoons" in The *Courier-Journal* directed against him over a period of six weeks. Much of the criticism was targeted at McConnell's refusal to make public the names of donors to the McConnell Center for Political Leadership at the University of Louisville. McConnell said he had never heard of any other senator every being subject to such an "intensive, obsessive" attack.

The *Courier-Journal* stood by its coverage and challenged McConnell to point out any mistakes in the paper's coverage of him. The paper then noted that McConnell did not produce a single error in their coverage.

But McConnell did turn to a familiar political tool to make his case: he conducted a poll. McConnell reported that "a majority of readers of The *Courier-Journal* believed that its political coverage had a liberal bias and that overall the paper was 'out of touch and irrelevant' and that 'those who read it most trust it least.' "

The paper's executive editor questioned the poll's methods, called its results "insignificant," and said the paper would continue to use the same standards to cover McConnell and every other political figure in the state.[70]

Rod Grams, then a Republican senator from Minnesota, was also running for reelection in 2000 when he launched an attack against the *Star Tribune* of Minneapolis. Grams' anger was aimed not at attack coverage, but lack of coverage. Grams' complaint was that the paper demonstrated its liberal bias by ignoring his accomplishments in the Senate.

Grams' campaign spokesperson Kurt Zellers sent an email to various media outlets attacking the paper's dedication to "running Rod out of Washington." Zellers wrote, "The *Star Tribune* has an agenda that is fundamentally different from that of a vast majority of Minnesotans—an agenda that supports the government over the people, servitude over self-determination and handouts over hard work.... The *Star Tribune* editorial page has become a satellite office of the Democratic National Committee."

Zellers asserted that that The *Star Tribune* "chooses to censor the Senator's activities" to the point that "if a voter relied only on The *Star Tribune* for information, they'd think Sen. Grams has been sleeping under a rock, when nothing could be further from the truth."

The *Star Tribune* answered back. In an article written by Eric Black, the paper noted that Grams "declines about 29 out of every 30 requests for interviews from The *Star Tribune*'s Washington Bureau." One of the paper's Washington bureau staff noted that he had "never covered a public official who makes it so difficult to find out what he's thinking and what he's working on. Not a week goes by that the Senate is in session that we don't ask for an interview with Grams.... We literally beg him and his staff for interviews to talk about his legislative priorities."

With Minnesota at the time represented by polar ideological opposites in the Senate, the paper's staff was very cognizant of the contrast in positions offered by Grams' and senior Senator Paul Wellstone. As Black noted, the paper was "painfully aware that the bureau writes more about Sen. Paul Wellstone than about Grams" but that the origin of the imbalance is the senators' behavior. "Wellstone, who is comfortable around journalists, overwhelms the bureau's reporters with access, which makes it easy for them to write about him.... If you need a quote to finish up your story, Wellstone will give you 10. Grams is the opposite."[71]

John Ashcroft of Missouri was yet another Republican senator to launch a public battle against a state newspaper in 2000. Ashcroft's dispute was somewhat more dramatic though. It was propelled by his decision to bar a *St. Louis Post-Dispatch* reporter from the bus that had been provided by his campaign to ferry reporters between twenty-five Missouri cities and towns on the senator's statewide campaign blitz.

The Ashcroft campaign announced it had thrown the reporter off the bus to protest the paper's "liberal bias." One specific article, published on October 26, 2000, which criticized the unexpectedly political nature of Senator Ashcroft's speech to a St. Louis area elementary school, was cited by the campaign as evidence of bias. The article quoted the school principal's explanation that he expected the senator to offer something of a civics lesson, and instead he delivered a partisan stump speech.

The *Post-Dispatch* reporter who was barred from the bus had not written the article about the school visit.

An Ashcroft spokesperson explained the campaign's feelings about the media. "We don't have any problem with the media," the spokesperson said. "We have a very clear problem with bias on the part of the *St. Louis Post-Dispatch.*"[72]

The three incidents serve to illustrate that this is a battle fought under quite uneven rules of engagement. The media can have the last word and powerfully shape the amount and nature of the coverage when a public official cries "bias." However, when they are drawn into these entanglements, they tend to fight with one hand tied behind their backs. When a senator calls a paper biased, wrong, or even immoral, the paper is loathe to respond in kind. Indeed, all three papers responded with some facts regarding their treatment of the senator or politicians in general, but none was willing to engage in the name calling or public pouting of their accuser. To respond at the same level as the accuser would be seen as unprofessional and even biased. But when one side is screaming and the other is calmly denying, it is the screaming that is easier to hear and to remember.

A TALE OF TWO NEWSCASTS

The portrayals of CBS News and Fox News Channel (FNC) offer another interesting vantage point from which to view the battle between those who see the media as biased toward liberals and those who do not. Against the former network are lobbed the suspicions of almost every believer in liberal bias, while the latter benefits from a savvy marketing of its product as the antidote to the bias that pervades everywhere else.

Lack of Conformity

One of the clear implications of the coverage of bias is that it is dangerous to be different. By covering a story in a different fashion or by covering a story in a different quantity, a media outlet is almost automatically placed in the position of having to justify its decision. In effect, it is asked to prove that bias did not affect its decision-making. Proving a negative, is, of course, nearly impossible.

The most prominent example of a media organization diverging from the pack in 2001 was the CBS Evening News' decision not to cover Representative Gary Condit and his association with missing intern Chandra Levy. When other networks and newspapers had made it their lead story, CBS had not mentioned the situation. CBS did not cover the story until Condit had been officially contacted by the police, and even then, CBS gave the story less prominence than any major media outlet.

The decision did not go unnoticed. As one newspaper account put it, "the program's early and ongoing disdain for the story has brought criticism."[73]

Throughout the period in which the Condit/Levy story was making headlines, CBS and its anchor Dan Rather were charged with bias, following the premise that they had decided not to cover the story to protect Condit, a Democratic member of Congress. *Newsday* noted CBS's "refusal to focus on a Democratic congressman in trouble" opened up the network to charges of liberal bias.[74] The *New York Times* quoted one conservative activist baying, "I think the only person across America who doesn't think Gary Condit is a suspect in this case is probably Dan Rather."[75] In addition to wall-to-wall coverage of the Condit story, Fox News Channel regularly provided updates on CBS's lack of coverage.[76] Still other reports noted the widespread coverage of the lack of CBS coverage as follows: "CBS' apparent lack of interest has become news itself on CNN and Internet reporting and gossip sites."[77]

Ironically, given the charges of liberal bias, Condit's political record is anything but liberal. Condit is not only rated as more conservative than the average Democrat in the House, Condit is rated as more conservative than the average House Republican by the National Taxpayers Union 2000 spending scorecard.

Don Hewitt, longtime producer of CBS' *60 Minutes*, responded to critics' assertions that CBS News' bias was evident in its decision not to produce more stories on the Condit/Levy situation: "I'm fascinated by your fascination with Dan Rather's lack of fascination about Chandra Levy."[78]

CBS News president Andrew Hayward commented on the implications of the attack on his news team's decision. Heyward argued that "this notion of some kind of rigid orthodoxy of conformity, that we're supposed to somehow all be in lockstep" is dangerous, and that we had reached a time when "if one program goes its own way and doesn't do what all the others are doing, that is somehow offensive or wrong—as opposed to allowing for a spectrum for editorial judgment and disagreement."

Heyward questioned why the networks and newspapers that had pushed a story with no facts and no clear conclusions were assumed to have done the right thing. "It's ironic that organizations that make a practice of excessive coverage got a pass." Heyward said. "I would have reserved more indignation for the other end of the spectrum."[79]

Dan Rather's position on the matter was that there was precious little news being reported on the situation. "When rumors, gossip, speculation and all this other stuff began swirling and other people began reporting it—frequently, I'm sorry to say, reporting it as fact—my question always was, and continued to be, what do we know on the basis of our own reporting," Rather explained.[80]

Rather is personally the target of much attention and criticism in the media bias discussion. As one *Houston Chronicle* article put it, "Rather is only the most blatant example of universal journalistic liberal bias."[81] Rather is subject to criticism, it seems, for every story CBS runs, and every story they don't run. He is criticized for things he says, as well as things he hasn't said. As The *Houston Chronicle* pointed out, people ranging from "paranoids on the right" to Fox News Channel anchor Brit Hume seem to be keeping a file on Dan Rather.[82]

When CBS projected George W. Bush victorious late on election night, Rather used a play on words referring to a Hemingway novel, saying on air "The son also rises." The next day, conservative talk radio was abuzz with anger that Rather had said the "sun will rise tomorrow," as if he were so disturbed by Bush's victory that he felt the need to reassure America that the world would not come to an end.[83]

Mike Rosen, writing in the *Rocky Mountain News*, called Rather and CBS "positively shameless in their anti-Bush, pro-Gore spin on daily events" and faulted Rather for repeatedly mentioning that Florida's Secretary of State Katherine Harris, who was guiding the recount process in Florida, was a Republican. "Rather uses 'Republican,' " according to Rosen, "as an epithet."[84]

For Rather and CBS there is precious little that can be done in the response to bias charges. Denials are dismissed as self-serving. Decisions made that support the bias charges are catalogued as just one more piece of evidence. Decisions made that seem to contradict the bias charges are noted for being rare and meant to throw critics off the track.

Fair and Balanced

By contrast, while CBS and Dan Rather attempt to put out the endless fires of bias allegations, one network news source has ceaselessly hyped its tendency toward fairness with vigor and ferocity, and to such a degree that the rest of the media largely help spread their message.

According to newspaper accounts, Fox News Channel "is bringing an alternative to the liberal manipulation of news and analysis to television. Fox's slogan is: "We report; you decide."[85] Its news is an "oasis of balanced coverage."[86] The network is "an antidote to . . . huge liberal bias on CNN and MSNBC."[87]

As Roger Ailes, former media wizard for Ronald Reagan and Richard Nixon, and current chief executive of FNC explained to a pliant audience of reporters, "I think there is an underserved audience that is hungry for fair and balanced news." Conservative Ailes, who heads the network owned by conservative Rupert Murdoch, and whose news staff is headed by openly conservative anchor Brit Hume, dismisses criticism that his network's slogans "We report; you decide" and "Fair and Balanced" are nothing but a flashy coverup of the network's deeply conservative roots and tendencies. Ailes says the notion of FNC as conservative is merely "spin."[88]

While many reports repeated Fox's slogans and congratulated the network as if by announcing a slogan it had achieved the slogan's claim, a few reporters questioned the sales pitch. Eric Black of the *Star Tribune* noted that over a five-month period, Republican voices outnumbered Democrats among Hume's interviewees by a ratio of eight to one.[89] When a *New York Times* reporter asked for an example of the balance in Fox news, a network spokesperson cited FNC's policy of emphasizing the crime for which an executed person was convicted, rather than the details of the execution process or public reaction to it.[90]

The great significance of perception and placement over reality has not gone unnoticed by other media outlets. Despite a lineup that "balances" its opinion shows with hosts from the far right and the center left, CNN felt the sting of appearing less fair than

Fox. With "fairness" having come to mean "conservative," CNN began talks with right-wing icon Rush Limbaugh to host a CNN program.[91]

FNC's antidote-to-bias marketing plan has been so successful that not only has it inspired positive coverage of the network, but in the sincerest form of flattery, it has been appropriated by other media outlets. When Oregon's *Portland Tribune* was recently launched with the financial backing of conservative activist Robert Pamplin, Pamplin announced that his paper would provide "fair and balanced news." Just as Fox has its CNN and CBS to complain about, Pamplin targets the liberal leanings of The *Oregonian*, the state's leading paper (and a paper that endorsed presidential candidates George W. Bush and Ronald Reagan). Pamplin explained, disingenuously, that he's not running the paper "to dictate what any person says or does. I just give the basic philosophy."[92]

READER FEEDBACK AND MEDIA DEFENSES

FNC's marketing based on bias simply acknowledges the deep interest and concern about bias the media find in the general public. When newspaper editors read the mail, the email, answer the phone, and even when they meet people on the street, they hear about bias. As Mike King of the *Atlanta Journal and Constitution* noted, the most frequent complaint of readers is "liberal bias. Anti-Bush. Democratic spin. Label it what you want, this tops the list. It did before the November election and it continues unabated. Readers smell bias in some of the most innocuous stories we write, as well as some of the most important. Many callers and e-mailers also are firmly convinced there is a conspiracy afoot . . . to look for stories that might discredit conservative politicians and opinion leaders."[93]

The editor of the *Pittsburgh Post-Gazette*, John Craig, picked up the phone early one Saturday morning at a time when most calls to the paper are complaints about late deliveries. Instead this caller "wanted to complain about the newspaper's 'liberal bias.' It is a phrase that I have heard 100 times a week during the past three months if I have heard it once." When Craig made the case for the paper's fairness, "she responded that we also had a bias against Christians and Christianity."[94]

And so it goes for editors across the country who are bombarded with complaints of "extreme liberal bias and hatred of conservative values."[95] Colorfully, a reader wrote to the "If You Ran the Newspaper" column in the *Star Tribune* to note that "You're a bunch of Socialists." (The paper responded that it had only one admitted socialist on the payroll).[96]

Gamely, many newspapers try to make the case that they are not biased. Although John Craig of the *Post-Gazette* made his pitch to the angry caller and to his readers, he feared that denying bias "will be whistling past the graveyard."[97] Nevertheless, newspapers and other media outlets sometimes tally the numbers themselves to make their case.

Mike King was moved by the number of complaints targeting his paper's coverage of the national party conventions to check the facts. King explains, "I went through the primary home-delivered *Constitution* edition for the week of each convention, beginning with Monday. I looked at the amount of news coverage . . . the kinds of stories, photographs and display. . . . The bottom line: There was little difference in coverage from Philadelphia and from Los Angeles. That's no accident, we planned it that way."[98] The *Tennessean* committed itself to equally sized photos and headlines of Al Gore and George W. Bush throughout the campaign season.[99] Concomitantly, Jeff Greenfield of CNN noted that coverage of Gore and Bush speeches on his network were timed with a stopwatch in an effort to be balanced to the minute in total coverage per candidate.[100]

This interest in fairness, as measured by exactly equal treatment, can have quite odd consequences. The *Kansas City Star* was unable to provide details to its readers in advance of a campaign visit to town by George W. Bush, due to last minute changes in the then governor's schedule. When Vice President Al Gore subsequently came to town, providing media outlets with plenty of advance warning, the *Star* purposely choose to bury the information on Gore to be "fair" to Bush. Later, the *Star* admitted, "In an effort to be fair, the paper ended up with two misses."[101]

Toward what gain are these efforts to defend their product? "Readers," as the *Christian Science Monitor* noted, "roll their eyes at protestations of fairness."[102] Mark Jurowitz in the *Boston Globe* raises the silly but powerful specter of the need for Democrats to complain in equal force to Republicans if bias charges are ever to be put to rest: "One election—or a whole slew of content analyses by the Committee of Concerned Journalists—will not quickly change minds at Fox, the Media Research Center, or among Republican partisans. But if enough Democrats start screaming about pro-Bush bias, we might have the ingredients for a truce that finally buries this non-issue and returns the focus to the more meaningful failures of American journalism."[103]

CONCLUSION: A BIAS FOR BIAS

Reporters are biased, newspapers are biased, television networks are biased, even the weatherman has a "bias toward bad-weather news."[104] Thus, one thing is perfectly clear in exploring the coverage of bias. One bias the media have is toward covering bias.

For those who believe in the charges, there is a responsibility to inveigh against the unfairness. For those who constantly hear the charges, there is a responsibility to share the complaints. Even for those who dismiss the charges, there is a compunction to respond to what they see as a misleading accusation. Taken together, regardless of their motive or personal inclination, there is a considerable amount of media space dedicated to the matter of the media's bias.

The significance of this tendency lies in the interplay between allegation and defense. Allegations are exciting and alarming. When the Natural Resources Defense Council announced in 1989 that our apples were poisoned by Alar™, a chemical fertilizer, the charge filled the airwaves and newspapers. Consumers were left to assume the apples were poison, for what purpose would anyone make this accusation unless it were true? Charges that apples are unsafe make for front page news—denials of the information, that is, everything is normal and there is no need to worry, do not. Moreover, when those denying the accusation were employed as spokespeople for apple growers, why would one even begin to consider believing their denial, when it was obviously self-interested?

The charges were made, well-publicized, and the nation reacted. Nervous parents poured apple juice down the drain. Supermarkets pulled apples, apple juice, and apple sauce from their shelves. Apple growers suffered losses estimated at hundreds of millions of dollars. Regardless of the reality that the apples were safe, the industry struggled to overcome quite literally poisonous imagery.

Analogously, when people scream about media bias, they make news. Fewer voices are mounting a defense of the media, and those voices are both less prominent, and as in the case of apple growers' spokespeople, they are less trustworthy since they have an obvious stake in denying the charges.

The media's situation is further complicated by the fact that some in the media have decided to bash their own product. It is as if a group of apple growers has joined the other side and announced their own product is unsafe.

Charges of bias get more coverage, include a greater diversity of voices, and feature admissions of bias from those in the media. Denials of bias get less coverage and are based more heavily on the conclusions of those who have an interest in protecting the media's credibility.

As Gans (1980) argues, those in the media have a tendency to see things as they are seen. In other words, there is little room for reflection or introspection on the job, which produces a default tendency to follow the popular tide of opinion and assumption. Charges of bias, then, have the media on an endless treadmill on which belief in bias brings charges of bias, charges of bias produce coverage of bias, and coverage of bias brings even greater belief in bias.

NOTES

1. Surely the only rival for this distinction is the federal government.

2. Foreign papers in the database were removed from the results.

3. The article was also coded no bias if each of the three indicators pointed to a different bias conclusion.

4. Gelfand, Lou. 2001. "Reader Says Three Examples Show Paper has a Liberal Bias." *Star Tribune*, July 15.

5. Gelfand, Lou. 2001. "Why Was There Higher Billing for Dayton?" *Star Tribune*, May 20.

6. Kahn, Joseph. 2000. "Schlesinger: Today's Leaders Don't Match Past Giants." *Boston Globe*, November 29.

7. Rosen, Mike. 2000. "Liberal Media's Notable Quotes." *Rocky Mountain News*, December 29.

8. Balz, Dan, David Von Drehle, Susan Schmidt, and Roberto Suro. 2001. "A War Leaves Its Questions; 'What Ifs' Will Long Haunt Both Sides in Fla. Struggle." *Washington Post*, February 4.

9. Saunders, Dusty. 2000. "Politics Keeps TV Audiences Laughing." *Rocky Mountain News*, October 26, 2000.

10. Krauthammer, Charles. 2000. "Does the Media Lean Leftward? It Certainly Does." *Newsday*, October 4.

11. Kelly, Jack. 2001. "Media Bias: Same Old Stuff, In Mainstream Outlets, Good GOP News is not Known." *Pittsburgh Post-Gazette*, July 8.

12. Jurkowitz, Mark. 2000. "The Media: Familiar Bias Charge Given a New Twist." *Boston Globe*, November 2.

13. Krugman, Paul. 2000. "Is Bush Using Bait-and-Switch Tactics?" *Denver Post*, November 2.

14. Thomas, Chris. 2001. "Media Bias? No, Except Toward Juicy Stories." *Arizona Republic*, January 22.

15. Garchik, Leah. 2001. "Jesse Ventura Plays the Blame Game." *San Francisco Chronicle*, May 16.

16. Campbell, Matt. 2001. "Media Obstruct Message, NRA Says; Panelists Believe Liberal Bias Routinely Colors Coverage." *Kansas City Star*, May 21.

17. Cobb, James. 2001. "Ideology Trumped All." *Los Angeles Times*, August 26, 2001.

18. "Arts and TV In Brief." 2001. The *Boston Herald*, August 20.

19. "Entertainment Briefs." 2001. *Chicago Sun-Times*, August 7; Mitchell, Sean. 2001. "Public Radio, Under the Influence." *Los Angeles Times*, May 27; Hines, Craig. 2001. "TV Networks and Poll Parsing." *Houston Chronicle*, March 3.

20. Dobbs, Greg. 2001. "Rate Cut Worthy of Better Play." *Rocky Mountain News*, July 8.

21. Minter, Jim. 2001. "Attack on Bush Unfair: Media's Credibility Taking Direct Hit." *Atlanta Journal and Constitution*, July 9.

22. Campbell, Kim. 2001. "Kennedy's George Bows Out Gracefully." *Christian Science Monitor*, March 8.

23. Ayres, B. Drummond. 2001. "Political Briefing; McConnell Says Paper Is Out to Get Him." *New York Times*, June 3.

24. Johnson, L.A. 2000. "Voting for Change." *Pittsburgh Post-Gazette*, December 27.

25. Rosen, Mike. 2000. "Liberal Media's Notable Quotes." *Rocky Mountain News*, December 29.

26. Wegan, Therese. 2001. "Stem Cell Research: No, Because it Harms Human Beings." *St. Louis Post-Dispatch*, July 18.

27. Krauthammer, Charles. 2000. "Does the Media Lean Leftward? It Certainly Does." *Newsday*, October 4.

28. Kurtz, Howard. 2000. "Are the Media Tilting to Gore?; Charges of Bias Hang Over Campaign Coverage." *Washington Post*, September 25.

29. Kurtz, Howard. 2000. "Are the Media Tilting to Gore?; Charges of Bias Hang Over Campaign Coverage." *Washington Post*, September 25.

30. Krauthammer, Charles. 2000. "Does the Media Lean Leftward? It Certainly Does." *Newsday*, October 4.

31. Will, George. 2000. "On the Wings of Inglory: The Mendacity of Al Gore's Pre-Election Campaign is Pertinent to the Post Election Chaos." *Pittsburgh Post-Gazette*, November 13.

32. Carr, Howie. 2000. "Media's Blatant Democratic Bias Begs Questions." *Boston Herald*, December 3.

33. Kelly, Jack. 2001. "Media Bias: Same Old Stuff, In Mainstream Outlets, Good GOP News is not Known." *Pittsburgh Post-Gazette*, July 8.

34. Rosen, Mike. 2000. "Networks' Bias Rather Obvious." *Rocky Mountain News*, September 1.

35. Samuelson, Robert. 2001. "Impartiality in Presenting the News." *San Diego Union-Tribune*, August 30.

36. Rosen, Mike. 2001. "Liberal Media Muddles Middle." *Rocky Mountain News*, July 13.

37. Tillotson, Kristin. 2000. " 'The West Wing' An Executive Briefing for Real Candidates." *Star Tribune*, October 15.

38. Chavez, Linda. 2000. "Who's Watching the Watchdog?" *Denver Post*, October 2.

39. Sandalow, Marc. 2001. "Everything's Right For Conservatives In Washington; Thousands Gathered at Annual Retreat Celebrate GOP Successes." *San Francisco Chronicle*, February 17.

40. Rosen, Mike. 2000. "Bush Indelicate but on Target." *Rocky Mountain News*, September 15.

41. Kelly, Michael. 2001. "Dem's Complaints about Media Bias Don't Ring True." *Dayton Daily News*, May 17.

42. Krauthammer, Charles. 2000. "Does the Media Lean Leftward? It Certainly Does." *Newsday*, October 4.

43. Kurtz, Howard. 2000. "Are the Media Tilting to Gore?; Charges of Bias Hang Over Campaign Coverage." *Washington Post*, September 25.

44. Daley, David. 2001. "Full-Court Press: Use or Be Abused? Where Exactly does Bush Fall in Media Bias Debate?" *Hartford Courant*, January 19.

45. Kurtz, Howard. 2000. "Are the Media Tilting to Gore?; Charges of Bias Hang Over Campaign Coverage." *Washington Post*, September 25.

46. Kurtz, Howard. 2000. "Are the Media Tilting to Gore?; Charges of Bias Hang Over Campaign Coverage." *Washington Post*, September 25.

47. Samuelson, Robert. 2001. "Impartiality in Presenting the News." *San Diego Union-Tribune*, August 30.

48. Krauthammer, Charles. 2000. "Does the Media Lean Leftward? It Certainly Does." *Newsday*, October 4.

49. Saunders, Dusty. 2000. "Jennings Wins Over Radio, TV News Chiefs." *Rocky Mountain News*, September 26.

50. Campbell, Kim. 2000. "In Tight Election, Charges of Media Bias Reign." *Christian Science Monitor*, November 3.

51. Jurkowitz, Mark. 2000. "The Media: Familiar Bias Charge Given a New Twist." *Boston Globe*, November 2.

52. McNamara, Mary. 2001. "Activist to Bush: Wait Till Voters Wake Up." *Los Angeles Times*, August 22.

53. Saunders, Dusty. 2001. "CBS Defends Late Entry to Levy Derby." *Rocky Mountain News*, July 30.

54. Black, Eric. 2001. "Media Watch; Analyst: For Propaganda, Look to U.S." *Star Tribune*, May 11.

55. Kahn, Joseph. 2000. "Schlesinger: Today's Leaders Don't Match Past Giants." The *Boston Globe*, November 29.

56. Black, Eric. 2001. "Media Watch; The Bad News is, There's Bias Everywhere." *Star Tribune*, March 9.

57. King, Mike. 2000. "Journalists, Readers Differ on What's 'Fair.' " *Atlanta Journal and Constitution*, December 23.

58. Much as a conservative candidate for Texas treasurer, Martha Whitehead, once campaigned for the office by attacking it, arguing it was unnecessary and should be abolished. Whitehead won the election in 1994, and within two years the office was abolished.

59. Alpert, Bruce, and Bill Walsh. 2000. "On the Hill: News from the Louisiana Delegation in the Nation's Capital" *Times-Picayune* (New Orleans), November 26.

60. Rosen, Mike. 2000. "Liberal Media's Notable Quotes." *Rocky Mountain News*, December 29.

61. Craig, John. 2001. "Of Opinions and 'Bias'; Why a Newspaper Takes an Editorial Stand and Sticks With It." *Pittsburgh Post-Gazette*, February 11.

62. King, Mike. 2001. "Addressing your Criticisms, Targeting our Flaws." *Atlanta Journal and Constitution*, July 7.

63. Ostrow, Joanne. 2000. "Happily Tuned In to Bush." *Denver Post*, December 27.

64. Kinsley, Michael. 2000. "Fess Up, Journalists." *Washington Post*, November 7. Charles Krauthammer nevertheless complains about the lack of conservatives as if it is a conspiracy, "It can't get any fairer than that. Complaints by conservatives about liberal bias at the *Times* will be reviewed and adjudicated by liberals at the *Times*. You'll have to forgive the *Times* if there are no conservatives in the loop, either as reporters or editors. They don't have any. After all, you can only take this diversity thing so far." Krauthammer, Charles. 2000. "Does the Media Lean Leftward? It Certainly Does." *Newsday*, October 4.

65. Thomas, Chris. 2001. "Media Bias? No, Except Toward Juicy Stories." *Arizona Republic*, January 22.

66. Scheer, Robert. 2001. "Bill's Excellent Adventure: Clinton's Presidency Achieved Much Despite All the Sniping." *Pittsburgh Post-Gazette*, January 25.

67. Teepen, Tom. 2000. "Election Evoked Worst in Everyone." *Baltimore Sun*, November 6.

68. Jurkowitz, Mark. 2000. "The Media: Familiar Bias Charge Given a New Twist." *Boston Globe*, November 2; Campbell, Kim. 2000. "In tight election, charges of media bias reign." *Christian Science Monitor*, November 3.

69. Elaine Chao was later tapped by the Bush administration to serve as the secretary of labor for the federal government.

70. Ayres, B. Drummond. 2001. "Political Briefing; McConnell Says Paper Is Out to Get Him." *New York Times*, June 3.

71. Black, Eric. 2000. "Media Watch; Silenced?; Grams Blames Bias for Coverage Gap; Reporter Faults Lack of Access." *Star Tribune*, August 31.

72. Kraske, Steve. 2000. "Reporter is Banned from Bus." *Kansas City Star*, November 3.

73. Morris, Phillip. 2001. "Rather's Reserve Serves CBS Well." *Plain Dealer*, July 24.

74. Paulson, Ken. 2001. "Chandra Is News, But Not the Only News." *Newsday*, July 26.

75. Rutenberg, Jim. 2001. "Why Dan Rather and CBS Limited Coverage of Levy Case." *New York Times*, July 23.

76. Saunders, Dusty. 2001. "CBS Defends Late Entry to Levy Derby." *Rocky Mountain News*, July 30.

77. Morris, Phillip. 2001. "Rather's Reserve Serves CBS Well." *Plain Dealer*, July 24.

78. Saunders, Dusty. 2001. "CBS Defends Late Entry to Levy Derby." *Rocky Mountain News*, July 30.

79. Saunders, Dusty. 2001. "CBS Defends Late Entry to Levy Derby." *Rocky Mountain News*, July 30.

80. Morris, Phillip. 2001. "Rather's Reserve Serves CBS Well." *Plain Dealer*, July 24.

81. Hines, Craig. 2001. "Rather Appalling Appearance, Response." *Houston Chronicle*, April 8.

82. Hines, Craig. 2001. "Rather Appalling Appearance, Response." *Houston Chronicle*, April 8.

83. "Literature, Talk Radio Don't Mix." 2000. *Buffalo News*, November 12.

84. Rosen, Mike. 2000. "Fox News Makes Widening Impact." *Rocky Mountain News*, December 22.

85. Rosen, Mike. 2000. "Fox News Makes Widening Impact." *Rocky Mountain News*, December 22.

86. Rosen, Mike. 2000. "Networks' Bias Rather Obvious." *Rocky Mountain News*, September 1.

87. Saunders, Dusty. 2000. "O'Reilly Talk Show a Hit for Fox News." *Rocky Mountain News*, November 8.

88. Rutenberg, Jim. 2000. "The Right Strategy for Fox; Conservative Cable Channel Gains in Ratings War." *New York Times*, September 18.

89. Black, Eric. 2001. "Media Watch; Bias on the Right and Left: You Decide; Study Pokes a Hole in Fox News' Boast of Fairness and Balance." *Star Tribune*, July 6.

90. Rutenberg, Jim. 2000. "The Right Strategy for Fox; Conservative Cable Channel Gains in Ratings War." *New York Times*, September 18.

91. "Arts and TV In Brief." 2001. *Boston Herald*, August 20.

92. Fost, Dan. 2001. "Twice-weekly Tribune Making a Run at Portland News Market; Wealthy Owner may be Guarantee of Staying Power." *San Francisco Chronicle*, August 1.

93. King, Mike. 2001. "Addressing your Criticisms, Targeting our Flaws." The *Atlanta Journal and Constitution*, July 7.

94. Craig, John. 2001. "Of Opinions and 'Bias'; Why a Newspaper Takes an Editorial Stand and Sticks With It." *Pittsburgh Post-Gazette*, February 11.

95. Cunningham, Brendan. 2001. "Stop Distorting the Truth About Presidential Election." *Buffalo News*, January 18.

96. Gelfand, Lou. 2000. "Sometimes We Must Explain Why We Used a Name; Sometimes, Why We Didn't." *Star Tribune*, November 12.

97. Craig, John. 2001. "Of Opinions and 'Bias'; Why a Newspaper Takes an Editorial Stand and Sticks With It." *Pittsburgh Post-Gazette*, February 11.

98. Edmonson, George. 2000. "Evidence Doesn't Point to Democratic Bias." *Atlanta Journal and Constitution*, August 26.

99. Campbell, Kim. 2000. "In Tight Election, Charges of Media Bias Reign." *Christian Science Monitor*, November 3.

100. Jensen, Elizabeth. 2000. " 'Nightline' Email Goof Renews Cries of Media Bias." *Los Angeles Times*, December 15.

101. Pepper, Miriam. 2000. "News Before Political Rallies was Hard to Find." *Kansas City Star*, October 29.

102. Campbell, Kim. 2000. "In Tight Election, Charges of Media Bias Reign." *Christian Science Monitor*, November 3.

103. Jurkowitz, Mark. 2000. "The Media: Familiar Bias Charge Given a New Twist." *Boston Globe*, November 2.

104. Safire, William. 2001. "Hype: The Worst Weather; When Big Bad Storms Don't Show, Who's to Blame?" *Pittsburgh Post-Gazette*, March 9.

CHAPTER 2

Reporters and Car Salesmen: Public Opinion on the Media

There was a time when the American news media was held in high regard. Three decades ago, the media was thought of as a trustworthy industry that brought us news in a fair and professional manner (Erskine 1970). Those days are gone.

In 1998 when Americans were asked for a one word description of the national news media, the most frequent response was "biased" (Pew Center 1998, 22). In the 2000 Gallup survey mentioned in the preface, newspaper reporters were believed to be honest and ethical by one fifth as many respondents as was the most trusted profession, nursing. Trust in the media can best be characterized as low and dropping (Fitzsimon and McGill 1995; Alger 1996; Graber 1997).

What has happened to trust in reporters is seen by many as inextricably linked to what has happened to trust in government and politicians (Cappella and Jamieson 1997). Robinson (1974) for example, found that coverage of Richard Nixon and the Watergate scandal exacted a price on the trust not only of Nixon, but of politicians in general, and of the media. Similarly, Robinson and Kohut (1988) found that Ronald Reagan's scandal-filled second term cost both him and the media credibility.

In part, this process is seen as a reaction to the disputes over the truth that inevitably well up during coverage of a scandal. Given conflicting versions of events from the media and from a leader, and with no avenue to judge information directly, the American people are left unsure of the truth and skeptical of both the messenger and the accused.

Alternatively, such an effect may reflect the capacity for distrust to breed distrust. As Patterson (1994) has argued, cynicism and distrust born in the Watergate and Vietnam era powerfully inform the attitudes of reporters even three decades later. Importantly, journalists' distrust is applied not with a fine artist's brush but rather with a paint sprayer, and is therefore ill-suited to root out isolated corruption, but ideal to spread discontent and distrust concerning the larger government system with which the media are inextricably linked. Even those who are inclined to trust the press in general express less confidence in the fairness of the media's coverage of politics (Ornstein and Robinson 1990).

Various studies have explored the question of who is inclined to distrust the media. One widespread finding is that people who distrust the media tend to have a distinct political point of view. Gunther (1988) found that people with polarized opinions on issues tend to have less trust in the media. Similarly, others have found criticism of the media predicated largely on partisan or ideological beliefs of the observer (Becker, Cobbey, and Sobowale 1978; Lichter and Noyes 1996; Dalton, Beck, Huckfeldt 1998; Dautrich and Hartley 1999).

The work of Gunther (1992) and Lord, Ross, and Lepper (1979) suggests that people with relatively extreme ideas feel a greater personal connection to political views and are therefore sensitized to negative portrayals of their beliefs. In the process, they attend to these negative depictions more than to positive or neutral coverage and conclude that the media must be biased against their beliefs.

More moderate observers, on the other hand, are less likely to closely observe the coverage of an issue, political event, or political leader with an eye toward rooting out the negative slant because neither the issue nor the slant is of particular interest to them. Asked to discuss the fairness of the media, such individuals are left without glaring examples of bias offensive to their political beliefs, and are therefore less likely to think the media unfair.

Interestingly, Gunther (1992) and others (Dalton, Beck, Huckfeldt 1998; Lord, Ross, and Lepper 1979) assert that the actual fairness of media coverage is not a significant factor in assessments of bias. In other words, the key determinant in assessments of bias is not what's in the newspaper, but who's reading it.

Some dispute this depiction of bias as being predicated on political extremity. Bennett, Rhine, and Flickinger (2001, 172) studied trust in the media in 1996 and 1998 and report that they "were particularly struck by the finding that ideology did not significantly predict opinion about the press's fairness. Evidently, claims that the news media systematically tilt leftward do not resonate at the grass roots, at least insofar as perception of the news media's fairness is concerned." Moreover, their data indicate partisanship was similarly unrelated to assessments of press fairness.

However, their finding may have more to do with the variables they considered than an actual lack of partisan and ideological effect on perceptions of the media. To wit, Bennett and colleagues include measures of approval of the president and Congress in their models, both of which turn out to be significant. Those who approved of Bill Clinton in 1996, for example, were much more likely to believe the media were fair than those who did not. Obviously, partisanship and ideology would be related to approval of Clinton, suggesting their effects were felt in multiple variables included in the model.

Other researchers have suggested that consumption itself is a significant component in response to the media. Schneider and Lewis (1985) and Robinson (1986) find that high use of the media correlates with a belief in media bias. This is thought to be related to the extremism finding. Again, people with stronger beliefs are more interested in politics, then consume more media, all the while attuned to instances of negative coverage.

As for demographics, some researchers suggest belief in media bias is not significantly related to variables such as sex, race, religion, income, and education (Robinson and Kohut 1988). Bennett, Rhine, and Flickinger (2001), however, find that more education correlates with greater belief in media bias.

Overall, scholars emphasize that perceptions of media bias are likely to be very unstable. As the targets of the media's scrutiny change, each new target will activate the distrust of his or her partisans and sympathizers. Moreover, this area may be one of the most highly subjective questions in all of politics (Stevenson and Greene 1980). In fact, researchers have found instances of the same coverage producing allegations of bias from people on opposing sides of an issue (Vallone, Ross, and Lepper 1985).

Nonetheless, belief in a biased media is all the more upsetting to people because of the third-person effect—in which media coverage is seen as having little influence over oneself, but great influence over the general public (Gunther 1998; Lasora 1992; Mutz and Soss 1997; Salwen 1998; Tiedge et al. 1991)—thus enabling a self-interested media to brainwash the masses.

TRUST IN THE MEDIA, 2000

To explore confidence in the media, the results of a Pew Research Center for the People and the Press poll have been analyzed. The Pew Research Center surveyed more than 1,300 Americans between October 4–8, 2000 to ask about their perceptions of media coverage, their political beliefs, and reaction to the presidential campaign.[1]

A first look at the results suggests the dire situation the media are in regarding public confidence. Table 2.1 shows responses to the question "How often do you think members of the news media let their own political preferences influence the way they report the news?" More than 88 percent chose often or sometimes, while just 1.4 percent chose never. In other words, the vast majority of Americans believe that the news they receive is not merely the facts or a fair and reasonable accounting of events, but instead frequently reflects the political beliefs of the journalist. Clearly, with such widespread support for that notion, the door is open for the American people to doubt media credibility on any issue at any time.

Interestingly, perceptions of coverage of George W. Bush and Al Gore were not as dismissive of the media's capacity to be fair. Table 2.2 shows that less than one quarter of respondents thought the media had been unfair in its coverage of Bush, and under one-sixth thought coverage of Gore unfair.

This disjuncture between overall notions of a biased media and the general belief that the two presidential campaigns were treated fairly suggests that perceptions of media fairness may have a longer time perspective than some have thought. Bennett, Rhine and Flickinger (2001) argue that conceptions of media fairness are inextricably bound to the immediate events the media cover. If that were the case, one would expect a close connection between the results in Tables 2.1 and 2.2. Calling the media biased, in essence, in Table 2.1, and then largely considering the media fair in covering the biggest story of the year suggests that respondents have made a judgment about the media's larger habits without having to tie that conclusion to immediate specific instances. This

Table 2.1
Confidence in Media Fairness

How often do you think members of the news media let their own political preferences influence the way they report the news...often, sometimes, seldom or never?	
Often	56.6%
Sometimes	31.6
Seldom	8.2
Never	1.4
Don't Know	2.2

N = 871

Table 2.2
Perceptions of Media Fairness in Covering Presidential Candidates

	Would you say the press has been fair or unfair in the way it has covered George W. Bush's election campaign?	Would you say the press has been fair or unfair in the way it has covered Al Gore's election campaign?
Fair	65.2%	74.1%
Unfair	24.6	15.1
Don't Know	10.2	10.8

N = 860

is in line with those who argue that assessing media fairness is such an overwhelming task that responses ultimately hinge not on any media behavior, but on larger political beliefs.

Nevertheless, this picture was further complicated when respondents were asked if the media were rooting for either presidential candidate. Here we again see widespread perceptions of bias. More than 70 percent believe the media are clearly rooting for a presidential candidate (Table 2.3). There is some dispute as to who that candidate is, with 23 percent believing Bush is the preferred candidate, and more than twice that responding that Gore is the preferred candidate.

Considering these results together, we again see support for the abstract nature of media assessments. People believe the media report in keeping with their personal beliefs. People believe that

Table 2.3
Who Is the Media Rooting for in the Presidential Election?

Who do you think most newspaper reporters and TV journalists want to see win the presidential election - George W. Bush or Al Gore?	
George W. Bush	23.0%
Al Gore	47.4
Neither	5.5
Don't Know	24.1

N = 871

the media root for the candidate of their choice. And people see no great evidence of either. As such, lurking beneath the surface for most respondents is a bias that dictates coverage, and for many, dictates coverage that benefits Gore, but that presumably is clever enough not to be immediately detectable.

WHO DISTRUSTS THE MEDIA?

Is bias in the media seen by people regardless of the interest in politics, their political beliefs, and their background? Or are there any common denominators that encourage conclusions that the media are not to be trusted?

Data are presented to allow comparisons on two key questions, that is, whether the media are following their own political opinions, and whether the media are rooting for Gore. Tables 2.4–2.11 show the percentages of respondents who said the media often or sometimes follow their own political views, and the percentage who said the media are supporting Gore. In Table 2.4, we see the response of those on the high end of various indicators of political interest and activity. In brief, results above the overall means (90.1 for overall bias and 47.4 for Gore support) suggest that high levels of these characteristics encourage greater belief in bias, while results below the overall means suggest that high levels discourage belief in bias.

Table 2.4 shows that four out of six indicators of political interest and activity produce higher levels of belief in media bias, while six out of the six indicators produce higher levels of belief in media support for Gore. For example, among those who said they had "Thought a Lot About Presidential Election," 92.4 percent said the media follow their own political beliefs, and 53.4 percent said

Table 2.4
Opinion on Media Fairness by Political Interest and Activity

	Media Influenced by Own Views (Overall Mean=90.1)	Media Favor Gore (Overall Mean=47.4)
Thought About Presidential Election (a lot)	92.4**	53.4**
Followed News About Presidential Election (very closely)	93.7**	53.6**
Interest in Politics (great deal)	89.8	58.3**
Planning to watch next Presidential Debate (Yes)	89.3	50.7**
Frequency of Voting (Always)	92.2**	49.8**
Plan to Vote in 2000 (Yes)	90.6**	47.6*

N = 872
*difference is significant, p < .01 using Chi-Square.
**difference is significant, p < .05 using Chi-Square.

the media were rooting for Gore. Even more stark, among those who said they followed news about the presidential election very closely, 93.7 percent said the media follow their own beliefs, and 53.6 percent said the media were rooting for Gore. These are extraordinary totals. Near unanimity in the belief that the media are biased among those with the greatest interest in political news, while a clear majority believes that that bias is toward Democrat Al Gore.

Taken together, Table 2.4 indicates that notions of media bias are higher among those who report greater interest in politics, greater consumption of media coverage, and greater likelihood of political activity.

For the media, this precludes the defense that perceptions of bias are driven by people who pay the least attention. More importantly for our system, it underscores the significance of this situation. The people who are calling the media biased are voting at a higher rate than those who consider the media fair. In other words, those with the highest confidence in the media as an information provider are less likely to use that information to participate in politics.

Table 2.5
Opinion on Media Fairness by Political Attitudes

	Media Influenced by Own Views (Overall Mean=90.1)	Media Favor Gore (Overall Mean=47.4)
Want most Representatives Re-elected (Yes)	88.5	54.7**
Want Representative Re-elected (Yes)	90.4*	49.0
Do Bush and Gore take different positions on issues (Yes)	91.0	53.1**

N = 872
*difference is significant, p < .01 using Chi-Square.
**difference is significant, p < .05 using Chi-Square.

Table 2.5 shows belief in bias for those who think most members of Congress should be re-elected, those who think their member of Congress should be re-elected, and those who think there are important differences between Bush and Gore on the issues. According to Bennett, Rhine, and Flickinger (2001), the first two measures are likely to produce significant differences, as those who are relatively trusting will support the reelection of representatives and be less likely to see the media as unfair, while those who are relatively dissatisfied and disinclined to trust will be against representatives and the media. Contrary to that expectation, pro-Congress responses do not have a dramatic effect on media trust. For both those who want members of Congress re-elected in general and those who want their member reelected, responses to media fairness are very close to the overall mean. Similarly, the question on Bush's and Gore's issue positions shows no great effect on media bias beliefs. These results suggest that reaction to the media is not a proxy for reaction to the political system as a whole. Those angry at the government are not particularly more likely to distrust the media, and those not angry with the government are not particularly more likely to trust the media.

Responses to the matter of whether the media are rooting for Al Gore are more consistent, however. In each case, those who respond positively to the Congress, and those who think there are important differences between Bush and Gore, are more likely to think the media are rooting for Gore. This is likely a manifestation

Table 2.6
Opinion on Media Fairness by Preferred Presidential Candidate

	Media Influenced by Own Views (Overall Mean=90.1)	Media Favor Gore (Overall Mean=47.4)
George W. Bush	95.2	67.0
Al Gore	85.6	33.2
Ralph Nader	84.2	31.6
Pat Buchanan	100	40.0

N = 872
Both columns statistically significant, $p < .01$ using Chi-Square.

of the vast partisan divide on this matter. Republicans, by virtue of their party's control of Congress, are more likely to want members of Congress re-elected, and Republicans, we shall see the in following results, are more likely to think the media biased.

Indeed, as Tables 2.6–2.9 illustrate, any way you look at it, Republicans are more likely to think the media biased. Table 2.6 shows that supporters of the two candidates of the right, George W. Bush and Pat Buchanan, considered the media biased at a rate of 95.2 and 100 percent, respectively. Against that near unanimity one can say "only" 85.6 and 84.2 percent of Al Gore and Ralph Nader supporters considered the media biased. More dramatic are the assessments of whether the media are rooting for Gore. Here we see a full two thirds of Bush supporters offering that conclusion. By contrast, one third of Gore supporters come to that conclusion.

As we saw in chapter 1, the media's case against itself is quite heavily weighted toward making the argument for a pro-liberal, pro-Democratic bias. These results indicate that message is hitting home, not with every voter, but with most, and with nearly all inclined to support conservative candidates. It does not really matter how one measures support for the liberal/Democratic side of politics; this difference in assessments of media fairness is constant. Table 2.7 breaks down the results by preferred vice presidential candidate, and Table 2.8 shows responses by preferred congressional candidate. Both tables indicate that Republican supporters are more likely to consider the media biased and more likely to conclude that the media support Gore. Considering partisan identification, rather than candidate preference, again produces the same pattern (Table 2.9).

Table 2.7
Opinion on Media Fairness by Preferred Vice Presidential Candidate

	Media Influenced by Own Views (Overall Mean=90.1)	Media Favor Gore (Overall Mean=47.4)
Dick Cheney	93.4	62.7
Joe Lieberman	88.1	38.1

N = 872
Both columns statistically significant, p < .01 using Chi-Square.

Table 2.8
Opinion on Media Fairness by Preferred Congressional Candidate

	Media Influenced by Own Views (Overall Mean=90.1)	Media Favor Gore (Overall Mean=47.4)
Republican	93.1	62.5
Democrat	87.2	37.2
Other	83.3	38.9
Don't Know	91.6	38.8

N = 872
Both columns statistically significant, p < .01 using Chi-Square.

While clearly Republicans are prone to see bias in the media, with Democrats less so, one interesting aspect of these data is the behavior of the independents and unaffiliated. In Table 2.6 we see that Nader and Buchanan voters are inclined to see things more like Gore voters than Bush supporters in regard to whether the media are rooting for Gore. With regard to preferred congressional candidate (Table 2.8), again those who are supporting a third party candidate or who are unsure who they are supporting resemble Gore supporters in their response to the media's preference for Gore. Finally, in the partisan identification results, again independents are closer in their views to Democrats than to Republicans.

This pattern suggests that assessments of media bias are far more influenced by the credibility of the messenger than by any meaningful evaluation of media performance, or even the political attention span of the consumer. In other words, strictly speaking, if the behavior of the media was creating these responses, Repub-

Table 2.9
Opinion on Media Fairness by Partisan Identification

	Media Influenced by Own Views (Overall Mean=90.1)	Media Favor Gore (Overall Mean=47.4)
Republican	92.3	67.0
Democratic	87.0	35.9
Independent	91.7	43.4

N = 872
Media Favor Gore statistically significant, p < .01 using Chi-Square.

licans, Democrats, and independents should have much the same response. The media are biased or they are not, but the three groups should agree. Conversely, if perceptions of the media were predicated solely on personal politics and the inclination to attend to information we disagree with, both Democrats and Republicans should see massive bias in the news because of the steady stream of two-sided information in the media, half of which is sure to offend them. Independents, non-partisans, and the like, on the other hand, should see far less bias than partisans because their perspectives should be less extreme, and therefore less coverage should offer propositions that offend them. Instead, what we see in the results is a Republican belief in pro-Gore bias, while Democrats and Independents both are less convinced. This suggests that the message of media bias, so often trumpeted by Republican leaders and carried forth by conservative columnists, resonates with those who identify with the right, while both the left and the middle are less moved by the argument.

In fact, when we consider the ideology of respondents, we see that it is the very conservative voter who most heartily embraces belief in media bias (Table 2.10). Almost 92 percent of very conservative voters believe the media follow their own political opinions, while an astounding 81 percent believe the media are rooting for Gore. Each step to the left, from very conservative to conservative, conservative to moderate, moderate to liberal, reduces belief that the media favor Gore. All the way to the left, at very liberal, belief in media bias rises, however. This corresponds to the existence of left-leaning critics of the media who make their case for media bias, albeit with less coverage than critics of the right.

A look at these results based on demographic characteristics

Table 2.10
Opinion on Media Fairness by Ideology

	Media Influenced by Own Views (Overall Mean=90.1)	Media Favor Gore (Overall Mean=47.4)
Very Conservative	91.9	81.0
Conservative	91.3	52.1
Moderate	88.8	40.5
Liberal	90.7	39.3
Very Liberal	90.2	46.3

N = 872
Media Favor Gore statistically significant, p < .01 using Chi-Square.

Table 2.11
Opinion on Media Fairness by Demographic Characteristics

	Media Influenced by Own Views (Overall Mean=90.1)		Media Favor Gore (Overall Mean=47.4)	
Sex	Men	90.4	Men	53.8
	Women	89.9	Women	41.8**
Race	White	90.3	White	49.4
	African American	91.1	African American	26.8
	Latino	86.4	Latino	47.8**
Religion	Protestant	90.0	Protestant	47.7
	Catholic	89.6	Catholic	44.9
	Jewish	73.3	Jewish	25.0
	Mormon	100	Mormon	100
	Other	98.3	Other	59.3
	None	88.7	None	43.3**
Income	Less than 20,000	83.7	Less than 20,000	43.4
	20-39,999	88.9	20-39,999	41.9
	40-74,999	91.3	40-74,999	48.0
	More than 74,999	93.8*	More than 74,999	57.5**
Age	Under 36	90.2	Under 36	50.4
	36-54	89.5	36-54	47.1
	Over 54	91.0	Over 54	45.8**
Education	Less than High School	85.4	Less than High School	37.6
	High School	86.7	High School	43.3
	Some College	93.2	Some College	47.9
	College Graduate	92.0*	College Graduate	53.6**

N = 872
*difference is significant, p < .05 using Chi-Square.
**difference is significant, p < .01 using Chi-Square.

shows relatively little in the way of differences in belief in the media's overall fairness (Table 2.11). On that measure, only income and education have a statistically significant pattern. To wit, higher income and more education are associated with increased belief in media bias. Belief in the media favoring Gore, however, shows a pattern in all six demographic traits measured. To wit, women, African American, Jewish, low income, less educated, older voters were less likely to believe the media favored Gore. These traits, of course, are suspiciously similar to a demographic breakdown of supporters of the Democratic Party.

Multivariate Test of Bias

To explore the relative significance of the previously discussed traits, a logistic regression model was created using the belief that the media are rooting for Gore as the dependent variable. Belief in the media favoring Gore was chosen as the dependent variable, as opposed to belief in biased media, or any other possible measure of media distrust, in order to maximize the variance of the response. That is, a model assessing factors that produce belief that the media are biased overall would be hampered by the near universal agreement with the premise. Belief that the media was rooting for Gore, conversely, was a sentiment shared by nearly half of the respondents. Included in the model as independent variables are measures related to interest in politics and the campaign (political interest, media attention, voting frequency), political preferences (partisanship, 2000 presidential preference, belief that the presidential candidates differ, ideology, support for Congress), and demographic traits (sex, age, income, education, race).

As displayed in Table 2.12, we can see that the model produces fairly robust results, with 76.5 percent of the cases correctly classified, and a Nagelerke $R^2 = .43$. As was suggested by the bivariate results, among the most significant factors influencing belief that the media favor Gore are basic political beliefs, including support for Congress, ideology, and 2000 presidential preference. In short, those who supported the Congress (controlled by Republicans), those who labeled themselves conservatives, and those who supported George W. Bush were all more likely to believe the media were rooting for Gore. Applying the coefficients suggests that someone with all three of those traits was 45 percent more likely to think the media were rooting for Gore than was someone with none of those traits.

Turning to the interest variables, we see that those who were high in media attention and voting frequency were more likely to conclude that the media favored Gore. Media attention, which was

Table 2.12
Belief in Media Favoring Gore Logistic Regression

	B	s.e.	Wald	significance
Political Interest	.81	.45	10.03	.07
Media Attention	6.21	3.14	23.80	.05
Partisanship	-.16	.17	.90	.34
2000 Presidential Preference	2.25	.64	16.99	.001
Ideology	-1.31	.58	17.68	.001
Candidates Different	-.45	.23	3.71	.05
Support Congress	-1.22	.24	25.93	.000
Voting Frequency	-.41	.14	8.25	.004
Sex	-.97	.23	17.11	.000
Age	.01	.01	4.66	.03
Income	.09	.05	3.85	.05
Education	.15	.07	4.35	.04
Race	-.50	.37	1.86	.17
Constant	4.42	1.54	8.25	.004

Note: Variable coding for dependent variable: Media Favor Gore (1 = yes, 2 = no). Variable coding for independent variables: Political Interest (0 = no interest in politics, campaign ads, or debates, 5 = high interest in politics, campaigns ads and debates); Media Attention (1 = no interest in seven topics, 14 = high interest in seven topics); Partisanship (1 = Strong Republican, 5 = Strong Democrat); 2000 Presidential Preference (1 = Buchanan, 2 = Bush, 3 = Gore, 4 = Nader); Ideology (1 = very liberal, 7 = very conservative); Support Congress (1 = yes, 2 = no); Candidates Different (1 = yes, 2 = no); Voting Frequency (1 = always, 5 = never); Sex (1 = men, 2 = women); Age (age in years); Income (1 = less than $20,000, 4 = more than $75,000); Education (1 = less than high school, 4 = college graduate); Race (1 = Non-African American, 2 = African American).

measured in a series of questions about level of attention to a wide variety of topical issues, shows that those who were paying the most attention to the media were 12 percent more likely to consider the media for Gore than those who paid average attention, and 18 percent more likely to consider the media for Gore than those who paid the least attention. Concomitantly, regular voting was associated with a 4 percent increase in thinking that the media support Gore compared to those who voted irregularly.

In addition to being conservative and relatively committed to politics and media consumption, those who thought the media were rooting for Gore can also be described as more likely to be male than female, more likely older than younger, more likely wealthy than poor, and more likely well educated than not.

IMPLICATIONS

The overall pattern of these numbers suggests two noteworthy conclusions. First, there is widespread belief that members of the media serve their own beliefs in their reportage. One must search for any group of people in which fewer than 85 percent agreed with the sentiment that the media are inflicting their beliefs on us. Indeed, there were not only few such groups, but few in those groups. Which is to say, the media could turn to Ralph Nader supporters for a relatively more optimistic outlook on their fairness, but even 84 percent of Nader's voters believed the media biased, and only 2 percent of the country voted for Nader.

Beyond its ability to cultivate distrust widely, the media must also be aware of the distinct and disquieting conclusion of a group of voters that the media favored Al Gore in the election of 2000. These sentiments, while by no means universal, were prevalent among conservatives and Bush supporters, and among those with a high level of political interest and media consumption. Such people are both politically offended and quite valuable customers. They are paying attention, and their attention is worth advertisers' dollars.

Long ago the partisan press died because its slanted coverage limited its market appeal to those with contrary views. Despite a long-standing economic imperative to produce neutral news, media outlets today find themselves almost thrust backward in time. For the media now, the central question may not be whether the media are biased, but whether they are perceived to be biased. A motivated, alienated constituency hungry for news is not going to endlessly consume newspapers and news shows that it considers slanted. No doubt this pattern has fueled the popularity of conservatively oriented talk radio (Barker 1998; 1999; Hofstetter 1998). And, in an age where technology is constantly opening new paths to news (on the Internet, on an ever expanding roster of cable news channels), the move toward conservative media outlets will likely continue. Ironically, the logical extension of the flight of conservatives from mainstream media is the rebirth of the partisan press.

NOTE

1. Pew Research Center for the People and the Press poll data can be accessed at their web site (www.people-press.org).

CHAPTER 3

The Jury Is Still Out: Academic Evidence on Media Bias

Read the many scholarly articles and books on media bias and you will be struck by the diversity of their conclusions. There are studies that find a clear liberal bias in the media, studies that find a clear conservative bias in the media, and to be sure, studies that find no bias in media.

Passions run high on this issue not just among the general public, but even among academics. When Efron (1971) published her indictment of the liberal media, which she titled *The News Twisters*, teams of scholars set out to show that the primary news twister was Efron herself. Stevenson and his colleagues (1973), for example, demonstrated that Efron's data were, to put it charitably, unreliable, or more pointedly, fictitious.

Overall, though, critics of this field of research lament that much of the work appears to be lacking in logic, in that conclusions are fit to the unique circumstances of the available data, or forged without the benefit of any evidence at all. Studies of certain media outlets that are not representative of any larger whole, or of specific years in politics that may have been particularly propitious for one party or the other, yield wildly different results and foster wildly unreliable conclusions. What is too often missing is a theory that guides both the search for evidence and its interpretation. Indeed, D'Alessio and Allen (2000, 135) comment that "there does not appear to be a major theorist of media bias."

Nevertheless, this chapter reviews the three major approaches to studying media bias. In the first section, we will see the results of surveys of reporters on their political preferences and opinions. In the second section, studies of the coverage of issues and political controversies will be considered. In the final section, research focusing on coverage of political campaigns and candidates is presented. While these studies will arrive at many different conclusions, considering them as a whole provides us with a strong sense of what researchers have been looking for in the search for media bias, and what they have overlooked.

REPORTERS AND THEIR OPINIONS

While attention to claims of media bias has certainly exploded in recent years, it is by no means a new source of concern. Dating back to the Roosevelt administration, Rosten (1937) showed that Washington reporters were more likely to vote for FDR in 1936 than was the general public. Indeed, Rosten found 64 percent support for Roosevelt among reporters, with some of those journalists opposed to Roosevelt (6 percent) preferring the socialist candidate. Follow-up studies have repeatedly found reporters to be more liberal than the general public (Rivers 1962; Hess 1981).

The Media Elite

One of the more prominent efforts to document the political proclivities of reporters was conducted by S. Robert Lichter, Stanley Rothman, and Linda Lichter. In their book, *The Media Elite*, they describe interviews with hundreds of journalists "at America's most influential media outlets" (Lichter, Rothman, and Lichter 1986, 20). The authors' sample includes writers and editors at major newspapers and newsmagazines, and reporters and producers for network television news. The authors explore the background and the political and social beliefs of media professionals.

Among the key numbers the authors point to: 54 percent of media professionals considered themselves liberals, while 17 percent labeled themselves conservatives. In presidential voting, at least 80 percent of the respondents reported supporting the Democratic candidate in each of the four prior presidential races. And on the issues, a majority supported Affirmative Action, abortion rights, the principle that homosexuality is not wrong, that environmental problems are important, and that government should reduce the income gap between the rich and poor. Indeed, "only 18 percent believe that working wives whose husbands have jobs should be laid off first, and even fewer, 10 percent, agree that men are emotionally better suited for politics than women" (31). Fifty percent of their media respondents said they had no religion. In sum, according to Lichter, Rothman, and Lichter, "These attitudes mirror the traditional perspective of American liberals" (30).

Moreover, the authors see a group far removed from the average American: "Substantial numbers of the media elite grew up at a distance from the social and cultural traditions of small-town middle America," lack religious commitment, and are "virtually unanimous in opposing . . . traditional constraints" on behavior (Lichter, Rothman, and Lichter 1986, 22, 31).

To further substantiate the point, *The Media Elite* offers the answers of business executives when asked the same questions that had been put to the journalists. The journalists were "to the left of business executives . . . on virtually every issue the survey addresses," with the gap in opinion on abortion, homosexuality, and income redistribution approaching 40 points (32–33).

Lichter, Rothman, and Lichter point out that liberals not only predominate among their overall media sample, but also among each age division of the sample. In fact, in a separate survey of journalism students, the authors found that the students held views on issues similar to those of working journalists, with the students being even more liberal.

Herbert Gans (1985) was sharply critical of the Lichter team's study for what he considered to be a standard that lent itself to exaggeration.[1] For example, Gans points out that when *The Media Elite* group claimed that 68 percent of journalists favor "income redistribution," the question journalists were actually responding to was "whether government should work to substantially reduce the income gap between the rich and the poor." Gans argues that someone answering affirmatively to that question might support job programs, training, or education efforts that would improve the economic prospects of the poor without necessitating a direct income redistribution plan.

Gans also considers the language used to be unnecessarily inflammatory: the media "are described as irreligious, hostile to business, and supportive of homosexuality and adultery, as well as of affirmative action" (1985, 30). However, Gans' strongest objection is the use of business executives as a comparison sample for reporters. "Why should journalists be compared to corporate managers," Gans asks, "when a more apt comparison would be to other employed professionals, like teachers, social workers, and salaried lawyers?" (1985, 31).

Lichter, Rothman, and Lichter's response to critics such as Gans was largely to point out how unremarkable their findings are when placed in the context of many different researchers using different questions and different samples, all of whom come to the same conclusion regarding the liberal/Democratic preferences of the media (for example, Wilhoit, Weaver, and Gray 1986; Johnstone, Slawski, and Bowman 1976). In fact, in subsequent years, researchers including S. Robert Lichter and many others have reaffirmed this tendency (for example, Beyle et al. 1996; Sabato 1991; Rothman and Lichter 1987).

89 Percent!

Allegations of liberal bias were amplified in volume and fervor in the aftermath of the 1992 election. A survey of Washington journalists found that 89 percent had voted for Democrat Bill Clinton in 1992, 7 percent for Republican George H.W. Bush, and 2 percent for independent Ross Perot (Povich 1996). Dennis (1997, 115) notes that these results were "trumpeted by conservative critics as proof positive of their worst fears."

Using the same data, Dautrich and Hartley (1999, 96–97) illustrate that reporters and even editors were much more likely to vote Democratic, call themselves Democrats, and consider themselves liberals than were the American people (Table 3.1). They also point to specific instances such as coverage of the 1994 Republican "Contract with America" issue agenda, where a majority of reporters admitted they covered the document as a campaign proposal and not a policy discussion (Dautrich and Hartley 1999, 100). Of course, Patterson (1994) would argue that reporters cover everything as a campaign proposal, and it is unrealistic to single out the treatment of one Republican plan. Nevertheless, Dautrich and Hartley find that not only are reporters more liberal than America as a whole, but that most admit their opinions affect their work (1999, 99).

That brings up a frequent criticism of this line of inquiry—that it is too far removed from the daily task of journalists. In other

Table 3.1
Political Preferences of Media and American People

Vote in 1992

	Washington Reporters	Newspaper Editors	American Public
Bill Clinton	89	60	42
George Bush	7	22	40
Ross Perot	2	4	18

Partisan Identification in 1995

	Reporters	Editors	American Public
Democrat	50	31	34
Republican	4	14	28
Independent	37	39	25

Ideology in 1995

	Reporters	Editors	American Public
Liberal	61	32	20
Moderate	30	35	34
Conservative	9	25	27

Source: Adapted from Dautrich and Hartley, 1999, 96–97.

words, demonstrating the leftward leaning tilt of journalists does not necessarily establish the leftward leaning tilt of journalism. Thus, Patterson and Donsbach (1996) extend the survey concept by asking reporters not only for their political beliefs, but also, how they would cover a particular story. In the process, they consider the degree to which political beliefs influence reporters' news sense.

Patterson and Donsbach surveyed both print reporters and broadcast reporters in the United States and in four other democracies. American journalists placed themselves at 3.3 on a seven-point ideology scale (from 1, liberal to 7, conservative), while they placed their audience at 4.5 on the same scale. United States journalists, the authors conclude, are "slightly left of center" or a "mainstream group with liberal tendencies" (Patterson and Donsbach 1996, 465). Nevertheless, the reporters saw no correlation between their ideology and the overall ideological tone of the newspaper or news broadcast they worked on.

To test the effect of their beliefs on their reporting inclinations, Patterson and Donsbach provided four scenarios for reporters to react to. In each case (industrial pollution, taxes, prisons, Third

World debt), the authors created a written summary of a situation and then asked for reporters' reactions on whether this situation should be covered and how it should be covered. For example, Patterson and Donsbach described a new set of proposals to regulate industrial pollution, and then asked whether these proposals were newsworthy. Then, they asked what headline would be acceptable—for example, would the reporter approve of "Chemical Industry Predicts High Cost and Little Effect from New Regulations?" Then, would a preferable photo to accompany the story be a picture of smoke from smoke stack, or a picture of an industry spokesperson speaking at press conference, or a graph showing that pollution is already down without the regulations, or a graph showing that the proposal will reduce pollution in future?

Overall, they found a "significant correlation between journalists' personal beliefs and their news decisions" (Patterson and Donsbach 1996, 455). Specifically, 68 percent of U.S. journalists made decisions consistent with their ideology. In this case, liberals chose to portray the regulations sympathetically, and conservatives to portray the companies involved sympathetically.

"The survey provides substantial evidence that partisan beliefs intrude on news decisions," Patterson and Donsbach argue (1996, 465), and that "vestiges of the old-time partisan press" are still alive (455). In sum, "As journalists go about the daily business of making their news selections, their partisan predispositions affect the choices they make, from the stories they select to the headlines they write" (466).

The authors do not argue that reporters are maliciously biased. In fact, they acknowledge that journalists "operate within organizations committed to the principle of partisan neutrality" (456) but "partisanship can and does intrude on news decisions, even among journalists who are conscientiously committed to a code of strict neutrality. The evidence presented in this article indicates that partisan bias occurs at measurable levels throughout the news systems of Western democracies" (466).

"Most of this non-objective reporting," they believe, "is not the result of a conscious effort to take sides" (466). Instead, "the influence is subtle, most of them probably do not recognize it. It flows from the way they are predisposed to see the world" (466).

In fact, Patterson and Donsbach worry that this bias is so deeply hidden from the surface that it exacerbates its effect. By denying the existence of bias and maintaining some level of self-deception

over the existence of bias, there has grown a "perceptual gap between journalists' self image and their actions, and it leads them
to reject any suggestion that they are politically biased" (466). As
such, "complaints from politicians are dismissed as self serving"
and as "attacks on the press's freedom and a threat to its objectivity" (466).

While the preponderance of academic voices on the question of
reporters' political beliefs agree with this study's assessment that
they are personally liberal, there are some who vigorously dispute
the notion. Robinson and Sheehan (1983, 296), for example, find
that "in their reporting and in their private interviews, none of
our reporters expressed anything approaching anti-system opinion. Most spoke as if they were 'moderates' or 'not very political.'" Even more frequently heard, though, is the objection that
personal political views do not dictate the coverage that reporters
produce.

Herbert Gans (1985, 32) proclaims, "Personal political beliefs are
left at home, not only because journalists are trained to be objective and detached, but also because their credibility and their paychecks depend on their remaining detached." Everette Dennis
(1997, 116) adds, "the notion that reporters are free to use the news
columns to propagandize for their personal passions is nonsense."

Members of the media, while acknowledging that many journalists are personally sympathetic to the Democratic Party, claim
that partisan reportage is highly unlikely because there are too
many professional incentives that demand ideological neutrality.
Richard Reeves (1997, 40–41) argues that journalists "are anxious
to preserve their own credibility" and "most cannot make a living
if they are not seen by sources, readers, viewers, and bosses as
trying to be fair." That is because producers and editors believe
bias is a threat to credibility, and ultimately, a threat to credibility
is a threat to profitability (Dennis 1997; Kurtz 1994).

Ultimately, then, surveys of journalists' personal beliefs must be
weighed against a long history of journalism studies that find
there is little connection between reporters' personal political beliefs and the final reporting that emerges under their bylines (Epstein 1973; Gans 1980; Roshcoe 1975; Sigal 1973; Tuchman 1978).
In fact, a greater connection has been found between the personal
beliefs of the executives and owners of media operations and the
final coverage (Coffey 1975; Mann 1974).

Sigal (1973) argues that a journalists' opinions are functionally eliminated from the reporting process. "Even when a journalist is in a position to observe an event directly, he remains reluctant to offer interpretations of his own," Sigal (1973, 69) wrote, "preferring instead to rely on his news sources. For the reporter, in short, most news is not what has happened, but what someone says has happened." Shoemaker and Reese (1991) suggest the possibility that even if reporters are liberal, and even if their beliefs do affect their work, it is by no means certain that that work will favor liberals. They find, instead, that some reporters attempt to compensate for their own preferences to such a degree that their work is deferential to the position they disagree with.

Patterson and Donsbach (1996) document the connection between reporters' attitudes and their news decisions, but they do so in a survey setting. Despite their declaration to document bias in reporting, they document bias only in an anonymous survey, not in actual reporting. To wit, reporters' commitment to objectivity in responding to a hypothetical situation for an anonymous survey could reasonably be expected to be less sincere than their professional commitment to uphold the standards of their profession and their employer.

Ultimately, the implications of a personal journalistic preference for liberal ideas or the Democratic Party are thoroughly disputable.

CONTENT ANALYSIS

Issues

Turning from studies of reporters to studies of reporting, we find neither a dearth of passionate conclusions nor anything approaching a consensus. Nonetheless, researchers have approached this task from numerous angles, many focusing on the portrayal of issues.

Olasky (1988a), for one, wrote a book-length study on media coverage of abortion. He finds rampant liberal bias, and characterizes the media as "a lap dog for the Abortion lobby" (chapter 15). However, he does this with no data to demonstrate liberal bias in coverage, or unfair coverage of abortion in any form. Instead, his is evidence of bias by assertion. By calling it unfair, it is unfair.

Olasky finds, like Lichter, Rothman, and Lichter (1986) and

Dautrich and Hartley (1999), that journalists are liberal, and that they overwhelmingly favor abortion rights. This, combined with a distaste for the coverage that emerges, substitutes for evidence of bias.

Olasky (1988b) expanded his criticism of the media in a follow-up work that screams "Harvard, Yale, and other universities founded by Christians now preach an atheistic gospel. A similar story could be told of some of the great newspapers of the land" (20). Indeed, according to Olasky, newspapers became suffused with "anti-Christian" sentiments and became obsessed with stories on topics that represented "an evil unfit for breakfast table discussion" (22). In fact, Olasky asserts, "many editors of the past century have tried to publish God's obituary" (31). Olasky, however, offers no comparisons to coverage of other religions, and no standard by which to ascertain whether coverage is in some way biased against Christians, or merely offensive to him.

Maurer (1999) found a liberal bias in the tendency of the media to denigrate the various accusers of President Bill Clinton. Again, there is no comparison provided of media coverage of Republican scandals, and no reasoning offered for establishing the appropriate or fair amount of denigration of characters who, in this case, included admitted liars.

Not surprisingly, the same basic technique has been used to assert a conservative bias in the media. Solomon (1999), for example, decries the conservative bias of the media evident in their coverage, or more accurately, their lack of coverage of hunger in the United States. Solomon describes the hunger issue and the struggles of 30 million Americans who live without adequate resources to feed themselves. He asks why this situation continually goes without coverage, and arrives at the conclusion that it is because the people who suffer do not fit into the demographic needs of media and their advertisers. According to Solomon, with a media product aimed at those with the high disposable incomes that advertisers crave, the suffering at the bottom of the economy is not viewed as an attractive story. Solomon concludes, "people fighting for economic human rights have always had an uphill battle for space in the mass media. Now the media terrain is titled against them more than ever" (1999, 41).

Like Olasky and Maurer, Solomon is armed with dismay, but not evidence. General disappointment with coverage is not evidence of bias, and the assertion that something is under-covered is nothing more than an unfalsifiable proposition. Since there is no evidence to support the assertion, there can be no logical means to defeat the premise.

Cirino (1971), who reached the same conclusion on hunger coverage almost three decades earlier, does provide comparative evidence on hunger coverage. He finds, for example, that in the three newspapers he studied over a period of six months, stories on entertainment outnumbered stories on hunger 226 to 1. Stories on accidents outnumbered stories on hunger 327 to 1. Cirino points out that when CBS aired a documentary on "Hunger in America" in 1968, the outcry over terrible living conditions among the poor inspired the Department of Agriculture to expand the food stamps program immediately. Therefore, he argues, the failure to cover this issue is of tremendous significance. Nevertheless, as unmistakable as his results are, they still leave open the question of what the "proper amount" of coverage might be. Surely there is no scientific standard of adequate coverage of the hunger issue, or of entertainment and crime, for that matter.

Thus the progression from dataless studies to studies that present some form of results is not always a step toward reliable and meaningful evidence. To wit, Sabato's (1991, 86–92) analysis of liberal bias in the media is notable for replicating many of the techniques media critics accuse the liberal media of using. For example, individuals Sabato agrees with are not labeled with any political description, while those he disagrees with are "left wing." Moreover, negative coverage of Republicans is evidence of partisan bias, while negative coverage of Democrats indicates only structural or "non-ideological" bias. Perhaps most memorably, Sabato offers the startling piece of data that 10 percent of all news stories are chosen to fit the liberal media's agenda. Importantly, Sabato offers this 10 percent figure without any shred of substantiating evidence whatsoever.

Hewitt (1996), studying media coverage of the issue of homelessness, faults the media for more frequently quoting Democratic sources on the size of the homeless population. Hewitt does not, however, establish that the Democratic sources were incorrect. Thus, according to his work's logic, the media would be biased for failing to quote one side's inaccurate information with the same frequency as the opposition's accurate information.

There are, of course, content analysis studies that offer not just conclusions and data, but meaningful evidence on bias. W. Lance

Bennett (1990) started a line of research on the concept of media indexing. Bennett hypothesized that media coverage of an issue was not so much tilted to the left or right, but set to encompass the range of government positions. In other words, when there is disagreement within the government, the media will include both sides in its story. When there is unity within the government, the media will emphasize that position to the virtual exclusion of other ideas.

Bennett found support for his theory in a content analysis of *New York Times* coverage of U.S. involvement in Nicaragua in the 1980s. Bennett found that when Democrats in Congress complained about the Republican Reagan administration's policies, there was coverage of that dissent. When Congress approved of or was silent about the administration's policies, then the president's view was the only view covered. Overall, Bennett found that *Times* coverage of U.S. Nicaragua policy was almost exclusively told through U.S. government voices.

Dickson (1994) followed up on Bennett's work with another study of *New York Times* coverage, this time of the American invasion of Panama. Analyzing 263 articles on the situation, Dickson also found that the newspaper allowed the government to "define and dominate the political debate" (815). Indeed, only 1 percent of speakers quoted spoke favorably of Panama's leader, Manuel Noriega. Meanwhile, the theme of Noriega as a drug-lord the United States must stop was transmitted without filter from the U.S. government into the paper.

While both Dickson and Bennett's studies were confined to one paper and one event, Zaller and Chiu (1996) took up the challenge of documenting the indexing effect over time. They consider coverage in *Time* and *Newsweek* of 35 foreign policy crises from 1945 to 1991. They also measure the opinions of members of Congress through congressional votes and speeches.

Considering the overall tone of the articles, Zaller and Chiu find a correlation of .6 to .7 between the coverage and the opinions in Congress. In sum, they "find strong evidence that reporters do . . . appear to wax hawkish and wane dovish as official sources lead them to do" (Zaller and Chiu 1996, 386).

Kuklinski and Sigelman (1992) examine the indexing area with attention to both foreign and domestic issues in their analysis of the coverage received by U.S. senators. Counting up network television news coverage received by senators from 1972 to 1988,

Kuklinski and Sigelman explore the determinants of the amount of coverage each senator receives. They find that leaders of the Senate and extremist voices in the Senate tend to be disproportionately covered. They also find, in contrast to the indexing research, that opponents of the president's policies do not necessarily receive equitable coverage. Instead, senate opponents of the relatively unpopular Democratic President Jimmy Carter received significantly more coverage than senators who disagreed with the popular Republican President Ronald Reagan (see also Entman 1989; Hertsgaard 1988).

Campaigns

In addition to analysis of issue coverage, coverage of political candidates, elections, and campaigns has been scrutinized in numerous studies. Considering their importance, ubiquity, and ease of comparison, it is not surprising that great effort has been expended on comparing the coverage received by Democratic and Republican candidates. Most often focusing on the parties' nominees for president, these studies provide a deep pool of information regarding the relative treatment of the two parties over time.

Individual studies range in result from those that allege "pronounced, sustained, and overt" bias toward the Democrats (Lichter and Noyes 1996, 212), to studies that find coverage of the two parties "remarkably balanced" (Domke et al. 1997, 718) to studies that find "the Republican Party received more and better coverage" (Stovall 1988, 446).

Despite the relatively common foundation on which these studies rest, there are remarkable differences in scope. There are studies that consider the coverage of one paper in one election and studies that consider multiple media outlets over multiple elections. Some studies have employed rulers and stopwatches to capture the exact amount of coverage in newspapers or on TV (for example, Hofstetter 1976). Others have created elaborate lists of positive words and negative words to characterize the tone of coverage (for example, Domke et al. 1997), and others have even codified the level of dignity afforded candidates when they are photographed (for example, Waldman and Devitt 1998).

One typical but thorough study is Hofstetter's (1976) analysis of media coverage of the 1972 presidential election between Richard Nixon and George McGovern. For Hofstetter, the point of his study was fundamentally to address the "growing apprehension by some Americans that the nation's news services are not to be trusted" (1976, 3).

To determine whether the media were being fair or biased, Hofstetter analyzed television news coverage (from the three major networks) of the campaign, the two candidates, and their parties between July 10 and November 6, 1972. In those 89 days, Hofstetter reports that the networks aired 4,349 stories relevant to American politics.

Overall, Hofstetter found that Democrat George McGovern received more coverage than Republican incumbent Richard Nixon. Conversely, McGovern running mate Sargent Shriver received less coverage than his counterpart, Spiro Agnew. Moreover, for both parties, the overwhelming tone of the coverage was neutral. That is, in almost eight in ten stories, negative points were balanced with positive points, or there was no positive or negative angle to the story at all. In effect, "most coverage was neutral or ambiguous" (Hofstetter 1976, 206).

Overall, Hofstetter argues, his work "certainly challenges studies that assert strong biases in favor of, or in opposition to, a candidate are present in news coverage" (1976, 50).

Similarly, Domke et al. (1997) conducted a massive content analysis of coverage of the 1996 presidential campaign and found that Republican challenger Bob Dole and Democratic incumbent Bill Clinton received quite similar coverage.

The authors examined campaign coverage in forty-three newspapers from March to November of 1996. Their sample totaled over 12,000 articles.

Domke and his colleagues tabulated the ratio of positive paragraphs written about each candidate to the number of negative paragraphs written on each. For Bill Clinton, the ratio was 1 positive for every 1.18 negative. For Bob Dole, the ratio was 1 positive for every 1.17 negative. When they considered the tone of coverage over time, they found that both candidates' positive coverage peaked during their parties' national conventions.

Domke's team characterized their results as clear evidence that Dole's frequent complaints of media bias against him and his party were off target (1997, 727).

While there are many individual studies that come to conflicting conclusions regarding the fairness of treatment of Democratic and

Table 3.2
Academic Articles on Media Coverage of Presidential Elections

Election Year	Number of Studies	Consensus on Media Tone
1948	2[a]	Pro-Republican
1952	7[b]	Neutral
1956	2[c]	Neutral
1960	4[d]	Pro-Democratic
1964	3[e]	Pro-Democratic
1968	3[f]	Pro-Democratic
1972	11[g]	Neutral
1976	3[h]	Neutral
1980	5[i]	Pro-Republican
1984	9[j]	Pro-Republican
1988	10[k]	Pro-Republican
1992	8[l]	Neutral
1996	4[m]	Pro-Democratic

[a] Berelson et al. 1954; Millspaugh 1949.

[b] Klein and Maccoby 1954; Batlin 1954; Higbie 1954; Blumberg 1954; Kobre 1953; Nollet 1968; Price 1954.

[c] Repass and Chaffee 1968; Nollet 1968.

[d] Westley et al. 1963; Stempel 1961; Nollet 1968; Danielson and Adams 1961.

[e] Repass and Chaffee 1968; Stempel 1965; Nollet 1968.

[f] Stempel 1969; Graber 1971; Stevenson et al. 1973.

[g] Evarts and Stempel 1974; Stevenson et al. 1973; Doll and Bradley 1974; Malaney and Buss 1979; Lowry 1974; Frank 1973; Hofstetter and Zukin 1979; Hofstetter 1978; Meadow 1973; Woodard 1994; Graber 1976.

[h] Einsiedel and Bibbee 1979; Woodard 1994; Friedman, et al. 1980.

[i] Woodard 1994; Robinson 1983; Robinson and Sheehan 1983; Stempel and Windhauser 1984; Stovall 1985.

[j] Moriarty and Garramone 1986; Stempel 1991; Windhauser and Evarts 1991; Woodard 1994; Robinson 1985; Mullen, et al. 1986; Clancey and Robinson 1985; Stovall 1988; Stempel and Windhauser 1991;

[k] Stempel 1991; Popovich, et al. 1993; Moriarty and Popovich 1991; Windhauser and Evarts 1991; Center for Media and Public Affairs 1988; Woodard 1994; Buchanan 1991; Stempel and Windhauser 1989; Kenney and Simpson 1993; Stempel and Windhauser 1991.

[l] McCord and Weaver 1996; Lowry and Shidler 1995; Cavanaugh 1995; Center for Media and Public Afairs 1992; Staten and Sloss 1993; Mantler and Whitman 1995; Fan 1996; King 1995.

[m] Murphy 1998; Center for Media and Public Affairs 1996; Waldman and Devitt 1998; Domke, et al. 1997.

Source: Adapted from D'Alessio and Allen, 2000.

Republican candidates, D'Alessio and Allen (2000) make the case that the best available evidence comes when we analyze the work of all those authors together.

D'Allessio and Allen (2000) therefore created a meta-analysis of fifty-nine studies focussed specifically on coverage of presidential elections. They include studies with data starting with the 1948 election and ending with the 1996 election.

With the analytical power of all those studies, D'Allessio and Allen report "no significant biases were found for the newspaper industry" (133), "biases in newsmagazines were virtually zero" (133), and there were no more than "insubstantial" differences in TV coverage (133). Table 3.2 summarizes the year by year findings of the fifty-nine studies.

While individual campaign years, or studies of individual papers, might yield indicators of imbalanced coverage, D'Allessio and Allen consider those results to be "random error" (149). In other words, in characterizing the whole of the media, any sample limited to a specific year, or to a specific set of media outlets, will likely provide a misleading picture of the media universe. Studying media coverage of the 1964 election, for example, would lead one to think the media were clearly biased against Republicans. Alternatively, it could have been an anomalous year due to the unpopularity of the Republican nominee, Barry Goldwater. Studying the 1984 election, conversely, would lead one to think the media were biased against Democrats. Again, it could have been the relative popularity of the Republican incumbent, Ronald Reagan, that produced unusual coverage during that year. Similarly, studies of specific media outlets sometimes find bias, but those outlets do not necessarily represent the whole of the media (See for example, Kenney and Simpson 1993; Blumberg 1954).

Thus, D'Allessio and Allen place their confidence in the broadest possible sample of media coverage. In combining these fifty-nine studies, encompassing forty-eight years of presidential election coverage, they find there is clearly "no evidence whatsoever of a monolithic liberal bias . . . at least as manifest in presidential campaign coverage. The same can be said of a conservative bias: There is no significant evidence of it." (148)

THE 50-50 STANDARD

D'Allessio and Allen's (2000) partisan comparison, as well as those of most researchers who have considered campaign coverage, is based on the presumption of a 50–50 fairness standard. That is, given that we have two major parties competing for office, fair coverage of those two parties and their candidates should be equal in amount, tone, and prominence. As D'Allessio and Allen (2000, 137) put it, "a two-party system, which produces two essentially qualified candidates, each campaigning at roughly the same level, should produce events, activities, and discussion in two roughly equal amounts. Thus, coverage should be roughly equal for each side, and any departure from a '50–50' split could be considered a consequence of some kind of bias."

In essence, given the assumptions that both candidates are working hard for coverage and both are qualified for the office, the resulting coverage should be equal. But is this assumption reasonable?

Are both parties' candidates likely to be working equally hard for press coverage? Hofstetter (1976) argues that one reason Richard Nixon was featured less prominently than George McGovern in 1972 is that Nixon did not make himself available to the media, while McGovern was ceaselessly available to the media. Indeed, assumptions of equal media effort would have been particularly off the mark in the 2000 primaries, where Republican contender John McCain invited reporters onto his campaign bus and held court for hours on end, while frontrunner George W. Bush limited press appearances to brief, pre-arranged encounters.

Moreover, were two candidates to make the same effort, their ability to successfully communicate a message would no doubt vary. Simon (1998), for example, describes the great contrast between the campaign appearances of Bill Clinton and Bob Dole. On the issue of crime, for example, Clinton would invariably speak with a phalanx of uniformed police officers behind his shoulder. If the media covered the event, the positive association between Clinton and the police was essentially unavoidable. By contrast, Bob Dole held crime events in such locales as California's Death Row. With the candidate uneasily walking the aisles of the state penitentiary, eyed by humans condemned to death, a reporter would be hard pressed to document the event in anything but unpleasant words.

Moreover, apart from effort and facility with the media, there is the question of qualifications. Why should candidates of varying ability, experience, and ideas receive precisely the same amount of coverage? Surely in the case of Richard Nixon, for example, who ran for president in 1960, 1968, and 1972, each of his major party opponents (John F. Kennedy, Hubert Humphrey, and George McGovern) was not his equal in all respects, nor were they precisely equals of each other. Thus it is hard to presume that the media should treat each of these candidates as the indistinguishable equal of Nixon.

Indeed, some researchers have concluded that while it is useful to document the relative coverage of the parties' candidates, the expectation that it be equal is not a reasonable standard on which to judge fairness (Kobre 1953; Stempel 1991).

UNFAIR BUT UNBIASED?

The confusion over a standard on which bias conclusions can be based has led some researchers to doubt the significance of the mountain of content analysis results that are available. Patterson and Donsbach argue that while content analysis "is useful in detecting tendencies in news coverage, it is limited in its ability to isolate and identify bias. It is exceedingly difficult to determine, for example, whether negative coverage of a politician or issue results from partisan bias, adverse circumstances, or other factors" (1996, 460).

To wit, there are a number of studies that find that coverage of candidates and issues is uneven, but not the product of bias. One category of such findings is the importance of the horserace in campaigns.

The conclusion that many studies of campaign coverage come to is that the popularity of the candidates is a driving force of the media's attention and emphasis. In their zeal to explain why winners win and losers lose, and in their exuberance to predict the outcome of future events, the media is powerfully influenced by the relative position of candidates in the polls.

Candidates who are leading are obviously good candidates running a good campaign, is the media's logic, and the resulting coverage reflects this truism (Patterson 1994). Candidates who are trailing have run a failed campaign, or do not have the characteristics necessary to be our leader, according to the same line of assumptions (Patterson 1994). Indeed, researchers have found horserace coverage is more prevalent than coverage of any other issue or topic during a presidential campaign (Domke et al. 1997).

Ultimately, a number of studies point to this ubiquity of

horserace coverage—in which the amount, tone, and subject matter of coverage is largely based on the candidates' positions in the polls—as a major factor that produces political coverage that may be unequal but is in no way based on the media's partisan or ideological preferences (on the 1972 campaign: Diamond 1978, Patterson and McClure 1976; on the 1976 campaign: Patterson 1980, Diamond 1978; on the 1980 campaign: Robinson and Sheehan 1983; on the 1984 campaign: Buell 1987; on the 1988 campaign: Jamieson 1992; on the 1992 campaign: Haynes and Murray 1998; on congressional campaigns: Clarke and Evans 1983).

Other researchers have pointed to the media tendency to continue covering what they have been covering. McCarthy, McPhail, and Smith (1996), for example, examined coverage of protest events in Washington, D.C. They found that the absolute size of the protest is the single biggest factor in predicting coverage. More people at a rally are more likely to be covered, and to be covered more thoroughly. However, the authors also found that preexisting coverage of the issue being protested was also an important factor. In other words, if protests on two different issues were to draw the same size crowd, the protest on the issue that had been getting more coverage in the past would be more likely to receive media attention. The authors suggest that while their results are not indicators of ideological or partisan bias, they instead support a basic inertia bias in the media (Gamson et al. 1992; Ryan 1991). It is easier to cover things that have been getting coverage. It is easier to sell editors on the need for another story on an issue than to convince an editor that a heretofore obscure matter needs attention.

Thus, McCarthy, McPhail, and Smith's (1996) evidence supports the view that there are structural biases not rooted in political beliefs that nevertheless have significant implications for how issues are covered. Similarly, Entman (1996) concludes that on a very partisan environmental battle waged in the Congress in 1995, the media's coverage was neither liberal nor conservative and neither fair nor useful.

Entman (1996) explored coverage of a proposal to curtail environmental regulations. In the 1994 Republican campaign platform, the Contract with America, party candidates pledged to conduct rigorous cost-benefit analyses of any future regulations on business, including environmental regulations. The clear effect of the proposal was to halt regulations relating not only to the environment, but also to work place safety. Using twenty-nine major newspapers, the three network television news shows, and news magazines, Entman analyzed six months of coverage of environmental and safety regulations during the period between the Republican victory in the election of 1994 and the first five months of their control of the House of Representatives.

In the hundreds of stories he reviewed, Entman found a strong negative reaction to the Republican proposal. News stories treated the proposal negatively by a three to one margin, while editorials were seven to one against the curtailment of regulations. Entman noted that words with negative connotations, such as "lobby" were more likely to be associated with proponents of the idea than with opponents. Meanwhile, health threat words received 25 times as much play as pro-economic phrases (employment, prosperity, wealth.)

While "the proposals raised important issues that thoughtful citizens should contemplate," Entman says his results show that the media failed to frame the issue to encourage rational debate (1996, 85). While they communicated a negative message about an idea they disliked, the media did not equip the American public with an understanding of the issue so that they would be able not only to determine their own preferences toward this bill, but to understand the larger issue and future priorities.

Much like James Fallows (1997) in *Breaking the News*, Entman argues that cynical dismissals of ideas only serve to underscore the American people's feeling of powerlessness. Instead of empowering them to come to a conclusion and then participate in the system to communicate what they want, people are left feeling uninvolved and insignificant. In fact, a number of studies have considered the media's tendency to undercut the electoral mandate of successful candidates by portraying their victories as personal or strategic rather than ideological triumphs (Hale 1993; Mendelsohn 1998; but see Entman and Paletz 1980; King and Schudson 1995) thus reducing the political imperative of electoral outcomes.

CONCLUSION

There is no shortage of conclusions, nor of contradictory conclusions, offered by academic studies of media bias. This much is clear, however: most researchers who have examined the political beliefs and practices of reporters find that they are either liberal or moderate. No academic study makes the case that the profession is dominated by right-wingers.

That may be where the consensus ends. Indeed, many question the significance of the political beliefs of the reporters in the ultimate reporting that they do. Thus, great efforts have been made to point out the political tendencies of our reporting, rather than just of our reporters.

Here there is little agreement. Many studies proclaim their bias conclusions without any meaningful data to substantiate their conclusions. Where data has been gathered to facilitate a meaningful comparison, researchers have generally found a tendency in the media to pay attention to the opinions of the two parties and to attend equally to the campaigns of the major party candidates. With many exceptions—perhaps traceable to the unique circumstances of the time, the candidates involved, or the media outlet being examined—studies of the larger situation tend to find little evidence of media bias.

This lack of consensus is taken as important evidence by Dautrich and Hartley (1999). They ask how the liberal bias of reporters can explain liberal bias in coverage if the balance of coverage constantly varies, while the liberal inclinations of reporters remain constant.

Instead of partisan or ideological bias, other researchers point to the horserace angle of coverage, where the popular candidate receives more and better coverage regardless of party or ideology. Others single out tendencies of the media that encourage them to pay attention to certain stories and simplify the issues they cover, which has the effect of making our news less useful, although not necessarily biased.

The problem that underlies all of this research, however, is the problem of the baseline. Olasky (1988a) says coverage of abortion is unfair, not by measuring it against any standard of fairness, but merely because he does not like it. Solomon (1999) says coverage of hunger is lacking, not based on any comparison or data, but merely because he thinks there should be more of it.

While these are extreme cases of researchers who offer no standard of what fair coverage might be, even those studies that have a standard of fairness have not logically justified it. Which is to say, one cannot begin to judge the bias of the media if there is no definition of what fair would be. And, one cannot meaningfully judge the bias of the media if the definition of fairness is arbitrary or based on plainly flawed assumptions.

Toward the end of providing logical evidence on bias, chapter 4 presents a standard of fairness and the results of a content analysis comparing the coverage of Republican and Democratic leaders.

NOTE

1. Gans' reaction is aimed at a previously published version (Lichter and Rothman 1981) of the same findings on which *The Media Elite* was based.

CHAPTER 4

An Objective Test of Partisan Media Bias

While there are millions of Americans, countless pundits, and a considerable number of scholars who believe the media are biased, even some of the most fervent media foes will admit that the devil is in the proof. Conservative activists Brent Bozell and Brent Baker (1990), for example, compiled every piece of evidence they could find that demonstrated the liberal bias of the media. They concluded that "media bias is real" and "prevalent" but that, alas, "there is no smoking gun"(4).

As chapter 3 described, the matter of media bias has been studied by various scholars using various techniques. But these studies have one thing in common: they lack an objective baseline from which to measure media bias.

METHODOLOGY: A BASELINE FOR COMPARISON

That is, studies on media bias have not been able to distinguish between unequal coverage and unfair coverage. After all, what really is fair coverage?

Previous studies have either offered no comparison and asserted bias merely by pointing out disappointing coverage, or offered a comparison that lacked a logical basis. For example, as was discussed in the previous chapter, a popular means of demonstrating fairness or bias in the media is to compare the coverage of Democratic and Republican candidates. But, is fair coverage treating two candidates or the two parties similarly? What if one of the candidates is more qualified? Should both candidates still get equal coverage? Is fair coverage presenting the range of the parties' opinions regarding a situation? What if one side is the position of most of our leaders and has the support of renowned experts?

Indeed, Hofstetter, author of a weighty study of coverage of the 1972 presidential election, admits that concluding whether or not the media are biased "in an objective and scientific manner is no simple and straightforward matter," because "the most vexing problem in studying bias is to discern a baseline for comparisons of news coverage" (1976, 189).

What is needed to make an adequate measure of bias is a logical and meaningful baseline on which to base a comparison. Comparison of random coverage of politicians cannot document bias, or the absence of bias, without some logical reason that would lead us to think that coverage should be the same.

Comparable Performance

This research offers a solution to the baseline problem. By focusing on situations in which political leaders from the two parties have produced comparable results or engaged in comparable behavior, we can test the media's reaction in a situation in which we can logically expect it should be similar.

In other words, instead of comparing, for example, the campaign coverage of Jimmy Carter to Ronald Reagan, or George H.W. Bush to Bill Clinton, comparisons that cannot help but be affected by enormous differences in the political acuity of each man, this study proposes to compare coverage of situations in which our leaders have produced the same results.

Using the unemployment rate, for example, we can see how the economy was covered under different presidents, and focus on situations in which they were logically entitled to the same coverage because they had produced the same result. Does a Democrat get better or worse coverage when producing the same result as a Republican? This is the key question in measuring media bias, and it will be answered here.

Importantly, this comparison can be made up and down the

political ladder in any situation in which a measure of performance or behavior is available. Thus for governors, both economic (unemployment rate) and crime (murder rate) coverage are utilized to compare treatment of Democrats and Republicans. For a comparison of mayors, crime coverage is also used. For the Congress, coverage of the 1992 congressional check bouncing scandal is used as an indicator of media fairness or bias.

Will evidence of partisan bias be found in these objective tests? Those who have studied reporters' personal opinions would predict there will be a pro-Democratic bias in the news, reflecting the political leanings of the reporters (Patterson and Donsbach 1996; Lichter, Rothman, Lichter 1986). However, those who have studied the larger news process would argue that the final product is overwhelmingly neutral because of the dictates of the profession, its value of "objective" reporting, its lack of tolerance for extreme perspectives, and the interaction of reporters with their supervisors (Gans 1980).

PRESIDENTIAL MEDIA COVERAGE

Using the unemployment rate as an baseline indicator to measure media fairness offers several advantages. Gallup polls consistently show the issue to be a major concern of Americans (Gallup Poll, 1986–1999). As such, researchers find that the economic performance of the country holds great weight in the voters' assessment of presidential performance (Bloom and Price 1975; Kernell 1977). And, there is a readily available set of results in the form of monthly federal unemployment figures. Using this approach, then, allows for a measure of coverage on a significant issue, and in situations in which the results of our leaders were equal. Therefore, their coverage should be equal.

For purposes of a partisan comparison, coverage of Republican President George H.W. Bush and his successor, Democratic President Bill Clinton, will be compared in situations in which the nation's unemployment rate was equal.

To achieve maximum reliability in the data, this examination goes beyond the national newspapers of note, which Shaw and Sparrow (1999) warn are often quite different in coverage and tone from the local papers most Americans typically read. As such, the study includes coverage from 150 newspapers nationwide, including at least two papers from every state in the country.

Papers were chosen for inclusion by state, with an attempt to include the largest paper in the state and a "typical" daily paper (in terms of median circulation of daily papers in the state). Fifty additional papers were chosen, where possible, to add a second typical paper from each state. If access to such a paper was not available, a paper from the same region of the country was selected.

Again, in an effort to produce maximum reliability in the data, four of the measures reported here are completely objective. Specifically, the number of articles published per month, the placement of the articles in the newspaper, the length of the article, and whether the president was mentioned prominently in the article are compiled. These indicators tell us how much attention the media are giving to the issue and whether the media are actively creating a link between the president and the issue. In situations where the rate is decreasing, more coverage, more prominent coverage, and closer association between the president and the issue are clearly desired. When these rates are increasing, more coverage, more prominent coverage, and closer association between the president and the issue are an obvious danger.

The tone of the article is also considered, based on a coder's estimation of whether the article was positive, neutral, or negative in its treatment of the president and the federal government. Specifically, articles were coded positive if they credited the president or federal government for a success, or credited either for trying to correct a problem. Articles were coded negative if they blamed the president or federal government for a problem, suggested the president had failed to respond to a problem or noted that either was uninvolved in a success. Articles that fit neither category, or suggested that both the president and the president's opponents were responsible for the situation, were labeled neutral.

The articles were rated on a three-point scale (1 = positive, 2 = neutral, 3 = negative) by twenty trained coders (each responsible for about 5 percent of the sample) who were unaware of the question being tested. A representative example of each follows: positive—"The key to this bright outlook was Clinton's success last year in winning congressional approval for tax increases and spending restraints to cut the federal budget deficit"[1]; neutral—"Even Bush's harshest critics would probably concede that not all the problems with the economy are his fault and that Congress bears a major share of the blame"[2]; negative—"Bush Camp's Incompetence on Economic Issues."[3] A subsample of the articles was reviewed by multiple coders, resulting in an intercoder reliability of over .8 for the tone estimate.

In theoretical terms, the significance of these measures is that they suggest the likely effects of the priming process. In short, when we are exposed to coverage of an issue, it has two important potential effects. First, coverage can encourage us to think that the issue is important. Second, coverage of an issue encourages us to think that our political leaders should be credited or blamed for the status of the issue. More coverage, more prominent coverage, and more closely established links between the political leader and the issue will all encourage priming (Iyengar and Kinder 1987). In other words, the significance of these measures is that they are likely to affect the popularity of the president, with more coverage of decreases in these problems helping to create a positive association with the president, and more coverage of increases in these problems helping to create a negative association with the president.

Coverage was examined during the period of February 1989 to September 1999, which includes all of the Bush administration and over six years of the Clinton administration. Searching the archives of the 150 papers for this period yielded 99,430 articles on unemployment (defined as use of the word unemployment in the headline, or first three paragraphs of the story). For each of those articles, whether prominent mention was made of the president (again using the headline or first three paragraphs of the story as the standard) was recorded. The placement and length were recorded for a random sample of 5 percent of those articles (4,971 articles), and the tone of the article was assessed by coders for a random sample of 1 percent of those articles (995 articles).

Results

Is there partisan bias in this coverage? Comparisons of coverage in months when Bush and Clinton had the same rate of unemployment[4] (which encompasses just under half of the months in the period studied) reveal little real difference on the number of stories, the length of coverage, the placement of coverage, mention of the president in the coverage, or tone of coverage (Table 4.1).

While unemployment under Clinton garnered about six percent more articles, those articles were about five percent shorter. Those

Table 4.1
Coverage of Unemployment When Democratic and Republican
Presidents Have Equal Results

	George H.W. Bush	Bill Clinton
Number of Stories on Unemployment Per Month (n=62)	768	812
Number of words per story (n=2512)	840	801
Percent of stories on front page (n=2512)	5	6
Percent of stories prominently mention president (n=50,774)	2.3	2.9*
tone of coverage (1=positive, 3=negative) (n=529)	2.3	2.2

Note: Based on coverage during the 62 months under study when Bush and
    Clinton had a matchable unemployment rate. The unit of analysis for the
    "Number of Stories" measure is the month, for the other variables it is the
    article.
*difference is statistically significant at p < .01, using Chi-Square.

stories were slightly more likely to be on the front page during
the Bush administration, but Clinton was slightly more likely to
be prominently mentioned. The tone of the articles on a three-
point scale (1 = positive, 3 = negative) was 2.3 for Bush and 2.2
for Clinton. In other words, in situations in which these presidents
from opposing parties produced precisely the same results, they
received very similar coverage.[5]

Indeed, on four of the five comparisons, the difference between
coverage during the Bush and Clinton administrations is statistically insignificant. The one exception, the number of stories that
prominently mention the president, achieves statistical significance based largely on the high number of articles included in the
comparison, rather than a politically meaningful difference in coverage.

Examples abound of what could best be described as typically
skeptical coverage received by these two presidents on economic
issues. James Risen, writing in the *Los Angeles Times* in 1994, offered an elaborate discussion of Bill Clinton's inability to receive
credit for improvements in the economy.

Working Americans to Bill Clinton: Yes, Mr. President, it's still the economy. But it's hard to believe in a recovery that you can't see or feel.

It has become perhaps the biggest puzzle in this extraordinary election season. The recovery appears to be in full swing but Americans aren't giving Clinton and his fellow Democrats much credit for it. If the economy is going so well, why are so many voters in such a foul mood?

Risen went on to discuss the possibility that the notion of economic expansion might be misleading.

For the typical American family . . . things aren't so great after all. The relatively robust growth of the economy and the drumbeat of positive economic reports emanating from Washington mask an underlying and far more troubling trend: American wages, benefits and living standards have continued to slide during the first two years of Clinton's presidency, even as many workers are putting in longer hours at less secure jobs.

Granted, American businesses are enjoying booming profits and surging productivity. But most of the rewards are going to a relatively narrow slice of the electorate—highly educated, affluent households—while the typical American family continues to tread water.

While the recovery has created millions of new jobs, at least half of them are . . . "soft jobs"—many are part-time or temporary, pay low wages or offer limited benefits.

Employment at temporary-service agencies as a percentage of the work force is at its highest levels in at least a generation, while the number of Americans with employer-provided health insurance fell from 62% in 1988 to 57% last year.

What's more, Risen argues, Americans are unwilling to acknowledge even genuine improvements in the economy.

Some findings seem to defy reality. Although the economy has created approximately 4.8 million new jobs since December, 1992, and the jobless rate has dropped from 7.6% to 5.9%, only 20% of those polled said they believe that the unemployment situation is improving.

All this leaving the Clinton administration in a precarious and defensive position.

Without widespread appreciation of his economic accomplishments, some analysts believe, Clinton becomes vulnerable to a host of other

voter concerns, from controversies concerning his personal affairs to
doubts about his leadership abilities.

This voter antipathy toward Clinton and his economic policies has the
White House frazzled. Many in the Administration believe that Clinton
has been denied the rightful political benefits that generally accrue to an
incumbent President during a period of solid economic growth.

Clinton aides tick off the numbers: three years of declining budget
deficits for the first time since the Harry S. Truman Administration, an
economy contributing more than twice as much to world growth as the
other six major industrialized nations combined and rapid job creation
combined with consumer inflation that remains below 3% per year.

"There are more than 4 million people out there working who weren't
working before Bill Clinton became President," said Alicia Munnell, as-
sistant Treasury secretary for economic affairs. "They have families, and
you'd think they would be happy. . . . But you don't even see that."[6]

The combination of skepticism about whether things are good,
and if they are good, skepticism that the president had anything
to do with the improvement, makes for a most difficult atmos-
phere for the president.

Indeed, George H.W. Bush faced a remarkably similar discussion of his economic record in a 1992 *Newsday* article.

It's confusing when economists say the recession is over. It doesn't feel
like it.

Technically, Bush points out, the national economy is on the mend
after being in a recession from the summer of 1990 to the spring of 1991.
But that is misleading. The economy isn't growing fast enough to create
jobs and that's what is hurting consumer confidence the most. While the
national unemployment rate has dropped slightly in recent months, from
7.8 percent in June to 7.5 percent in September, it didn't drop because
more people found work; it fell because people gave up looking for
work.

Prospects for quick improvement are slim. New layoffs are announced
almost weekly and consumer confidence is still dropping. The housing
market, a traditional engine of economic growth, is in the doldrums despite the lowest mortgage rates in decades. And, like a ticking time
bomb, the federal government's accumulated debt—$4 trillion—keeps
growing at a rate of nearly $1 billion a day. Some economists even fear
that the country might slide into another recession.

The article undercuts not only the notion that there has been
any improvement, but also any claim Bush might have to contributing to the improvement.

Right now, the economy has been growing for five consecutive quarters, but by such small amounts that it isn't producing new jobs as quickly as old ones are lost in areas such as defense. In an ordinary recovery, the economy grows at a rate of about 5 or 6 percent. In this recovery, growth is barely 2 percent.... And so, while an economics professor might disagree, it still feels like a recession.

Bush cites both the low inflation and low interest rates as evidence of his successful economic management. But the independent Federal Reserve Board, not the president, plays the biggest role in affecting inflation and interest rates.[7]

President Bush did not do himself any favors, however, with his tendency to alternate between inexplicable indifference and uncontrollable panic when discussing the economy. Consider these descriptions of Bush from December 1991 and January 1992.

The headlines in Texas that day last December when George Bush was coming to visit were all about an impending layoff at a General Motors plant near Dallas. Across the country, the news was about the recession. Unemployment was rising. America was worried ... Bush had a working man's lunch of chicken-fried steak, corn and mashed potatoes with seven hard hats building a highway interchange. When the $48 tab arrived, the President of the United States, scion of upper-crust Greenwich, Conn. in the winter and Kennebunkport, Me. in the summer, took out an impressive shock of bills. "Of course I'm buying," he said. "I'm loaded."

In that instant, in six words tossed off in jest at the Cafe 121, a roadside hamburger joint, George Bush encapsulated perhaps the most crucial oversights of his presidency: The failure to recognize the impact the recession was having on the fortunes of the nation and its potential impact on his own political fortunes.[8]

A month later, his tone had changed radically. In a speech in New Hampshire, Bush told his audience he cared about the economic situation they were facing, in fact, he summed up his concern literally with the words, "Message: I care."[9] The extent of the economic slowdown was no longer something he was going to deny. "I probably have made mistakes in assessing the fact that the economy would recover.... I think I've known, look, this economy is in free fall. I hope I've known it. Maybe I haven't conveyed it as well as I should have, but I do understand it."[10]

Despite his new hyperbolic stance on the economy, later that same day Bush responded to a question about his willingness to extend unemployment benefits to workers affected by this economy in "free fall" by telling a nervous worker, "If a frog had wings, he wouldn't hit his tail on the ground—too hypothetical."[11]

Overall, in thousands of articles on Bush and Clinton the basic conclusion was similar. They took heaping blame for the bad, and generally faint praise for the good. This was not an indictment of a Republican president, or a Democratic president, but a common element of their existence. Indeed, the data paint a clear picture of two presidents being treated quite similarly—which is not necessarily to say fairly, or reasonably—but equitably with respect to the treatment received by the other.

GUBERNATORIAL MEDIA COVERAGE

Next we turn to a comparison of media coverage of Democratic and Republican governors. Given the similar centrality of the economy for governors as presidents (Carsey and Wright 1998; Atkeson and Partin 1995), again the unemployment rate is utilized to gauge performance. Crime is also a significant factor in the evaluation of state chief executives (Levitt 1997). Thus, the murder rate in the states will also be used as a baseline from which to compare coverage.

In an effort to broaden the comparison utilized in the presidential discussion, examination of gubernatorial coverage will focus not just on one Democrat and one Republican, but a total of 100 Democratic governors and 100 Republicans governors from across the country. Coverage of fifty Democrats and Republicans who had comparable unemployment rates will be compared, and coverage of fifty Democrats and fifty Republicans who had comparable murder rates will be compared.

To make such a comparison, the annual murder and unemployment rates for all fifty states, as well as the change in those rates, were gathered for each state during a twenty-year period from 1977 to 1996. Working backwards from 1996, governors were paired with the chronologically closest governor from the other party whose rate and rate change were comparable. Only cases where the incumbent governor was in office for the period of measurement and the reporting of the rate are used (that is, articles written on rate changes that took place during a previous administration are not utilized). The overall rate and the rate of change were considered comparable if both figures were within .1 for a pair of governors (with the unemployment rate expressed as "out of 100," and the murder rate expressed as "out of 100,000." Governors for whom there was no comparable case to be paired with were excluded from the study.

This technique was performed once for the murder rate and once for the unemployment rate. Fifty pairs of governors were then randomly selected from among those with comparable unemployment rates and from among those with comparable murder rates.

Coverage of each pair was assessed by comparing newspaper coverage on the issue in the thirty days subsequent to the announcement of the relevant rate. Newspapers included in the Newspaper Abstracts and Nexis index services were used, resulting in the inclusion of articles from more than fifty newspapers (the newspapers include national, regional, and local papers). Articles from these newspapers during the appropriate period that mentioned the governor and the relevant rate or focused on the general situation in the state were gathered. This resulted in an average for the 100 pairs of governors of three usable articles per governor.

As was the case in the presidential comparison, three of the measures reported here are completely objective, specifically, the placement of the article (front page or inside), the length of the article, and whether the governor was mentioned in the headline of the article are considered.[12]

The tone of the article is also considered based on a blind coder's estimation of whether the article was positive, neutral, or negative in its treatment of the governor. Again, articles were coded positive if they credited the governor for a success or for trying to correct a problem (example: "Governor circled the globe to encourage investment"). Articles were coded negative if they blamed the governor for a problem, suggested the governor had failed to respond to a problem, or noted that the governor was uninvolved in a success (example: "Mismanaged several state agencies that are supposed to nurture job creation"). Articles that fit neither category or suggested that both the governor and the governor's opponents were responsible for the situation were labeled neutral (example: "Engler Cites Tax Cuts, But Democrats

Table 4.2
Coverage of Murder Rate When Democratic and Republican
Governors Have Equal Results

	Republican Governor	Democratic Governor
Front Page	20%	18.5%
Length of Article	2.0	2.1
Headline Mentions Governor	36.5%	39%
Tone of Article	1.9	2.1

N = 50 pairs

Credit National Economy"). A subsample of the articles was re-viewed by a second coder, resulting in an intercoder reliability of .84 for the tone estimate.

Results

The average treatment of Republican and Democratic governors in comparable situations is presented in Tables 4.2 and 4.3. Table 4.2 shows the averages for coverage when the murder rate is comparable. Only 1.5 percentage points separate the proportion of articles on Democrats on the front page from the proportion of Republicans, a statistically insignificant difference (using Chi-Square, $p < .10$ as a benchmark). The length of these stories is nearly the same, with the average being 2.0 (on a scale of 1–3) for Republicans and 2.1 for Democrats. As for the governor being closely associated with crime, Democrats are 2.5 percent more likely to be mentioned in the headline. The tone of the articles is also nearly indistinguishable for Republican and Democrats. Overall, the four indicators do not reveal a pro-Democratic bias, or suggest bias of any kind as all four partisan differences are substantively and statistically insignificant.

The results for coverage of unemployment are largely consistent with the murder rate results. The proportion of articles on the front page differs by only .5 percent. The length of stories indicator is the same for Democrats and Republicans. And the tone estimate, which slightly favored the Republicans in the murder data, here slightly favors the Democrats.

One measure, the proportion of headlines that mention the gov-

Table 4.3

Coverage of Unemployment Rate When Democratic and Republican
Governors Have Equal Results

	Republican Governor	Democratic Governor
Front Page	15.5%	16%
Length of Article	1.7	1.7
Headline Mentions Governor	16.5%	18.5%*
Tone of Article	2.0	1.9

N = 50 pairs
*difference is statistically significant at p < .10, using Chi-Square.

ernor, is higher for the Democrats by a small, but statistically significant margin. However, caution should be taken in interpreting
this result. While in isolation from the rest of the data, this ratio
would seem quite useful for Democratic governors and perhaps
suggest partisan bias in the coverage, one must consider this result
in light of the other seven comparisons offered. First, the dominant finding when considering all eight comparisons is that the
media treat Republican and Democratic governors in comparable
situations with quite remarkable equality. Second, statistical significance is a useful tool in suggesting whether a numerical difference is meaningful or not, but its results require interpretation.
Here, by applying the .10 standard to eight different comparisons,
there is clearly the chance for an erroneous significance finding
due simply to random luck. Thus, considered in the context of all
the comparisons, the data provide no meaningful evidence of partisan bias in newspaper coverage of Democratic and Republican
governors.

MAYORAL COVERAGE

To compare media treatment of mayors, the data include coverage of mayors in eight cities (with populations over 500,000) that
have elected Democratic and Republican mayors in the last twenty
years. The eight cities are New York, Los Angeles, Houston, Dallas, Indianapolis, Columbus, Charlotte, and Cleveland.

Here the focus is on crime, an issue considered to be paramount
in evaluation of mayors (Levitt 1997; Howell and Marshall 1998).

Again, the murder rate is used as a measure of outcome. For the purposes of this study, annual FBI statistics on city murder rates offer an ideal source of information for making a comparison between coverage of mayors when their administration's effect on the murder rate is comparable.

Depending on the city, there were between one and three newspapers available for analysis. All newspapers that were electronically searchable and featured a local section dedicated to city politics were included, although results have been weighted to equalize the importance of each city in the analysis.[13]

Coverage was examined during the period of January 1, 1980 to December 31, 2000. Searching the archives of the newspapers for this period yielded 1,886 articles on the mayor and the city murder rate/murder problem (or other synonymous phrases such as homicide rate). For each of those articles, coders determined whether prominent mention was made of the mayor (using mention of the mayor in the headline or first three paragraphs of the story as the standard) and the placement of the article (page number). For a random sample of half of the articles (943 articles), coders assessed the portrayal of the effectiveness of the mayor.

As was the case in the presidential and gubernatorial studies, the effectiveness of the mayor measure is based on a coder's estimation of whether the article was positive, neutral, or negative in its treatment of the mayor and the city government. Articles were rated on a three point scale (1 = positive, 2 = neutral, 3 = negative) by thirty-one trained coders (each responsible for about 3 percent of the sample), who were unaware of the question being tested. Again, articles were coded positive if they credited the mayor or city government for a success or credited either for trying to correct a problem (example: "Mayor Martin O'Malley's pledge a year ago to make the streets safer is showing measurable results.")[14] Articles were coded negative if they blamed the mayor or city government for a problem, suggested the mayor had failed to respond to a problem, or noted that either was uninvolved in a success (example: "City Hall was 'fiddling around while the murder rate climbed.' ")[15] Articles that fit neither category or suggested that both the mayor and the mayor's political opponents were responsible for the situation were labeled neutral (example: "In several large cities, murders and some other violent crimes have shown their first increases in years. Just as there was no agreement on what factors deserve credit for the decade's crime

Table 4.4
Coverage of Mayor by Partisanship

	Mayor Prominently Mentioned (n=1846)		Placement of Article (n=1846)		Effectiveness of Mayor (n=943)	
	DEM	REP	DEM	REP	DEM	REP
Reduced 10% or more	35	31*	6	5	1.2	1.2
Reduced 5-9%	32	30	6	7	1.4	1.3
Reduced 1-4%	21	19	8	9	1.7	1.6
Less than 1% change	5	6	9	9	2.1	2.1
Increased 1-4%	15	16	5	6	2.4	2.2+
Increased 5-9%	22	20	3	3	2.8	2.8
Increased 10% or more	27	25	3	4	2.9	2.8

*difference between Democrat and Republican total is significant using Chi-Square (p < .05)
+difference between Democrat and Republican total is significant using t-test (p < .05)
Note: Mayor prominently mentioned is percentage of all articles in which mayor is mentioned in headline or lead paragraphs; Placement of article is the average page number of the articles; Effectiveness of mayor is a three point scale (1 = positive, 2 = neutral, 3 = negative).

drop, there will be little agreement on why that trend is now leveling off, except for the truism that every society will be plagued with a certain irreducible minimum of mayhem.")[16] A subsample of the articles was reviewed by multiple coders, resulting in an intercoder reliability of over .9 for the effectiveness estimate.

All comparisons are made between mayors who have produced comparable results. Coverage of mayors for each city in each year was sorted into seven groups based on their relative effect on the murder rate (reduced 10 percent or more, reduced 5–9 percent, reduced 1–4 percent, less than 1 percent change, increased 1–4 percent, increased 5–9 percent, increased 10 percent or more) according to FBI statistics.

As Table 4.4 illustrates, there are few meaningful differences between the coverage of Democratic and Republican mayors. Ideally, a mayor would want great personal prominence in coverage of improvements, great exposure for those stories, and a positive tone. A mayor with an increasing murder rate would prefer less coverage, less prominent coverage, and of course, less negativity in that coverage.

Given these desires, neither the Democrats nor the Republicans seem to be benefiting from media bias. The one pattern that stands out is that mayors presiding over decreasing murder rates enjoy more positive coverage than those whose rates are increasing. This pattern is, however, evident for both Democrats and Republicans.

Looking at the prominence of the mayor, we see that, overall, Democrats are slightly more likely to be mentioned in the headline or lead paragraphs of the story, but that difference fails to meet measures of statistical significance in six of the seven categories (using Chi-Square, $p < .10$ as standard). Democratic and Republican mayors are more likely to be prominently featured in the best and worst categories and less likely to be highlighted in the middle categories.

Where the article was placed also shows very minimal differences between Democrats and Republicans. Again, Democrats overall have the slightest "edge" over Republicans in article placement, but the differences are quite small and, again, not sufficient to establish a statistically significant distinction. This edge, of course, is not an advantage when sharing negative news. Thus the Democrats are—by the slimmest margin—benefiting from more prominent positive news, and suffering from more prominent negative news.

The portrayal of the effectiveness of the mayor is most clearly affected by the cities' crime results. A declining murder rate all but eliminates negative stories about the mayor's crime record and decisions. A stable murder rate produces the most neutral coverage, and not surprisingly, an increasing rate produces the most negative coverage. This is again true for both Democrats and Republicans, with Republicans benefiting from a small but inconsistent advantage in the tone of the coverage. In four of the seven categories, Republicans receive more positive coverage, and in one instance that difference is statistically significant. However, the overall pattern, considering all seven categories, is again one of strong similarity in coverage of the mayors of both parties.

Taken in sum, these numbers suggest that a good record produces better coverage and a bad record produces worse coverage irrespective of the partisanship of the mayor. Despite the great hue and cry over partisan bias, this objective comparison of coverage offers no evidence of a partisan bias in the news media.

CONGRESSIONAL COVERAGE

Given the difficulty of linking a policy outcome to a specific member when dealing with a legislative body as opposed to an official in an executive office, a different indicator of performance was required to make a meaningful comparison of congressional coverage. The House banking scandal of 1992, however, offers a member-specific indicator of behavior, and one that was of great significance to the voters.

The House Banking Scandal

The House banking scandal of 1992 first came to light in a 1991 General Accounting Office (GAO)-audit that found that, in a one-year period, members had bounced over 8,000 checks in their House of Representatives bank accounts. The House bank, which was really the payroll office of the House with some bank functions, honored those checks without penalty, requiring only that sufficient money be placed in the account during the subsequent month. In effect, the House bank gave check-bouncing members one-month loans paid for with the funds of other House members.

When the GAO report was published in the Capitol Hill newspaper *Roll Call* on September 19, 1991, innocent members, primarily Republicans, began their calls for an investigation into the matter. Two weeks later, the House voted to have the Ethics Committee investigate the bank. Attention and pressure mounted over the ensuing months, stoked by members uninvolved in the check bouncing practice. On March 13, 1992, the House voted to disclose the identity of members who bounced checks. In April, the Ethics Committee released the list of members, revealing that 61.4 percent of sitting House members had bounced a check in the examined period (July 1988–October 1991). Seeking to diffuse the situation and calculating that the information would eventually be released, over 200 members had previously confessed to bouncing checks before the list was made public.

The leading check bouncer was Representative Robert Mrazek (D-NY), who had written over 900 checks with insufficient funds in his account. There was a tendency for younger, less wealthy, and Democratic members to bounce more checks. However, the practice was found among all ages, stations, and parties in the House (Stewart 1994). Indeed, then Minority Leader Newt Gingrich (R-GA) and House Speaker Thomas Foley (D-WA) were both on the check bouncing list.

While the true significance of the house banking scandal, which did not cost taxpayers any money, can be questioned, scholars argue that the situation held symbolic significance. Stewart (1994, 521) believes that the check scandal became "a filter through which issues of democratic accountability were examined." Others pointed to the diminution of "reputations for fiscal probity" caused by the banking scandal (Clarke, Feigert, Seldon, and Stewart 1999, 81). Given concerns about the overall economy and the growing budget deficit, the check scandal was ideally timed to create headaches for members (Jacobson and Dimock 1994), and was seen by pundits as "tantamount to an 8.0 shock on the Congressional Richter scale" (Alford, Teeters, Ward, and Wilson 1994, 788)

Though the precise findings vary somewhat, there is unanimous agreement among scholarly studies that the House bank scandal affected congressional careers. Decisions to retire and election strategy were affected by bounced checks (Alford, Teeters, Ward, and Wilson 1994; Anju et al. 1994; Clarke, Feigert, Seldon, and Stewart 1999; Groseclose and Krehbiel 1994; Jacobson and Dimock 1994). Moreover, in keeping with findings suggesting scandals typically cost members about 10 percent of the vote (Peters and Welch 1980; Welch and Hibbing 1997), the House bank scandal is associated with a significantly greater chance of losing in a reelection bid (Alford, Teeters, Ward, and Wilson 1994; Jacobson and Dimock 1994). While members attempted to explain away the bounced checks as minor oversights, it was clear that most Americans believed the practice was a deliberate choice of members. In an October 1991 poll, 83 percent of respondents said members bounced checks "because they knew they could get away with it," rather than doing so by mistake.[17] By April of 1992, when the list of check bouncers was made public, disapproval of Congress had reached a record high.[18]

Thus, bad checks, ironically, were far more important politically than were matters of larger, big picture consequence. In the words of Jacobson and Dimock (1994, 622), "The scandal ended many more congressional careers than had policy disasters such as the

savings and loan debacle, which left taxpayers holding the bag
for hundreds of billions of dollars, or the quadrupling of the national debt from $1 trillion to $4 trillion in little more than a decade."

Media coverage of the House bank scandal was intense. Headlines trumped the effects of the scandal ("Approval of Congress
Hits All-Time Low,"[19] or "Bad Checks Bouncing Against Incum-
bents in the Polls")[20] and took members to task for their lack of
responsibility ("Guess Who Bounced 8,331 checks in One Year,"[21]
and "Public Calls Lawmakers Corrupt and Pampered.")[22] Was this
coverage fair? Did members receive their scathing rebukes or mild
reproaches without regard to their party?

The same 150 newspapers utilized in the presidential comparison were again consulted. A search was conducted for articles on
members of the congressional delegation from the paper's state
who had bounced one or more checks. Articles were chosen for
analysis when a member was the focus of the article, rather than
peripherally mentioned or merely placed in a list. Specifically, a
count was made of the number of articles in which the member
was mentioned in the headline or lead three paragraphs of article,
and the percentage of those articles that mentioned the member's
banking record. Among the articles that mention the banking
scandal, further analysis was performed to measure the placement
(page number), length (word count), and tone of the article.

The tone of the article is considered based on a coder's estimation of whether the article was apologetic, neutral, or condemning in tone toward the member. The articles were rated on
a three-point scale (1 = apologetic, 2 = neutral, 3 = condemning)
by twenty-two trained coders who were unaware of the question
being tested. Specifically, articles were coded apologetic if they
suggested the member was an infrequent check bouncer (relative
to other members), or if they argued that the members had done
nothing wrong (example: "Among San Diego County's Representatives, Rep. Ron Packard, R-Carlsbad, has said he only wrote four
bad checks and Rep. Randy Cunningham, R-San Diego, has said
he only wrote one. Their records contrast sharply . . . and their
level of wrongdoing is a different order of magnitude" from
chronic check bouncers).[23] Articles were coded negative if they
faulted the member for being irresponsible with money, taking
advantage of the rules, setting a poor example, or being a particularly flagrant abuser of the House bank (example: "The House

Table 4.5
Coverage of Bounced Checks by Party

	Democrats	Republicans
% stories on checks (n=10,906)	16.2	15.8
Placement (n=1766)	8.8	9.1
Length (n=1766)	746	759
Tone (n=883)	2.4	2.2*

*difference is significant a p < .05 using a two sided T-test.

Ethics Committee listed her as one of the worst abusers of the House Bank.")[24] Articles that fit neither category, suggested a combination of apologetic and condemning responses, or attempted to explain the practices of the House bank without excusing the behavior, were labeled neutral (example: "Several congressmen sought to make a distinction between 'bouncing' checks and merely being overdrawn. Rep. Bill Thomas (D-Bakersfield), whose district includes part of the Antelope Valley, said: 'Have I bounced checks? No. Have I written checks which triggered overdraft protection under the so-called bank? The answer is yes.' "[25]) A subsample of the articles was reviewed by multiple coders, resulting in an intercoder reliability of over .8 for the tone estimate.

Coverage was examined from September 19, 1991 to November 3, 1992, which represents the period from the first mention of the scandal in the media to the subsequent election day. Searching the archives of the included newspapers yielded an average of forty-one articles per member (10,906 articles total). Using a computer search conducted on those articles, coders determined whether mention was made of the banking scandal, which resulted in 1,766 articles for analysis. For each of those articles, the placement and length was noted. For a random sample of half of the articles (883 articles), coders assessed the portrayal of the member's role in the bank scandal.

If partisan bias does exist, we should expect to see one party receive more coverage and more blame for their check writing habits than the comparison group.

For purposes of comparison, members were separated into eleven separate cohorts of check bouncers, each containing those who had bounced a comparable number of checks. An attempt was also made to keep each cohort at a similar total size.[26]

Table 4.5 presents the comparison of coverage of Democratic

and Republican check bouncers. Here, once again, we find little meaningful partisan difference. With regard to the number of stories on bounced checks, the placement of those stories, and the length of those stories, coverage of Democrats and Republicans was nearly identical. In other words, Democrats and Republicans who had engaged in the same behavior received much the same exposure from the media. The only category that reaches statistical significance (p <.05, using a *t*-test) is the difference in tone, which very slightly *favors* Republicans.

Overall, just as was the case in the presidential, gubernatorial, and mayoral results, this analysis of coverage of Democratic and Republican members of Congress provides no evidence of partisan bias.

CONCLUSION

The data presented here represent the first comprehensive evaluation of partisan bias using an equitable baseline with which to compare coverage. In the simplest terms, the finding is this: In a comparison of coverage of two presidents, 200 governors, the mayors of eight cities, and 266 members of Congress, all matched to a member of the opposite party who had the same outcome in office, there is simply no evidence for partisan bias.

In comparing coverage of presidents, governors, mayors, and members of Congress, different groups of newspapers from across the country were included and different issues were utilized as the basis of comparison. Regardless of the group of papers assessed or the issue compared, the overriding conclusion regarding partisan differences is that they do not exist.

What few indicators show any distinction between Democrats and Republicans are uniformly small in scope and inconsistent in direction. That is, the few measures that revealed a difference were slightly favorable to Republicans in some cases and slightly favorable to Democrats in other cases.

The results call into question the thrust of the media's coverage of itself, which tends to suggest that partisan bias is pervasive (chapter 1). The results call into question the thrust of public opinion, which tends to suggest that the media root for Democrats (chapter 2). And, the results call into question much of the scholarly research on this question which has not utilized a fair baseline with which to compare coverage (chapter 3).

Nonetheless, the lack of partisan bias does not preclude other, no less significant biases, from affecting media coverage. This is the subject of chapter 5.

NOTES

1. *Washington Post*, February 15, 1994.
2. *Houston Chronicle*, August 17, 1992.
3. *San Francisco Chronicle*, October 30, 1992.
4. This occurred at the rates of 5, 5.2, 5.3, 5.4, 5.5, 5.7, 5.9, 6.4, 6.6, 6.7, 6.8, 6.9, and 7.
5. Are reporters almost required to be fair to the parties since this is an issue with such clear and available data? That would be quite unlikely, according to Patterson (1994), who finds evidence of reporters forcing details to fit into the "story" they had in mind, even on issues such as unemployment.
6. Risen, James. 1994. "Voters Reluctant to Credit Clinton for Recovery." *Los Angeles Times*, October 24.
7. Kessler, Glenn, and Karen Rothmyer. 1992. "Can Any of These Guys Fix the Economy?" *Newsday*, October 11.
8. Gerstenzang, James, and Douglas Jehl. 1992. " '92 National Elections." *Los Angeles Times*, November 5.
9. Dowd, Maureen. 1992. "Immersing Himself in Nitty-Gritty, Bush Barnstorms New Hampshire." *New York Times*, January 16.
10. Dowd, Maureen. 1992. "Immersing Himself in Nitty-Gritty, Bush Barnstorms New Hampshire." *New York Times*, January 16.
11. Dowd, Maureen. 1992. "Immersing Himself in Nitty-Gritty, Bush Barnstorms New Hampshire." *New York Times*, January 16.
12. The front page and headline measures are both reported as percentages (i.e., the percentage of stories on the 25 governors that were on the front page.) Due to differences in how the databases express the length of articles, the length of the article measure is reported using a three-point scale (1 = less than 6 column inches, 2 = between 7 and 18 column inches, 3 = more than 18 column inches).
13. Newspapers utilized include *Daily News, New York Post, New York Times; Los Angeles Times; Houston Chronicle; Dallas Morning News, Fort Worth Star Telegram; Indianapolis Star; Columbus Dispatch; Charlotte Observer;* and *Cleveland Plain Dealer.*
14. *Baltimore Sun*, December 8, 2000.
15. *Philadelphia Daily News*, July 20, 1998.
16. *Columbus Dispatch*, December 26, 2000.
17. *New York Times*, October 10, 1991. Only 9 percent believed the bounced checks were the result of members having made mistakes.

18. *New York Times*, April 2, 1992.

19. *Washington Post*, March 20, 1992.

20. *Washington Post*, October 30, 1992.

21. *Washington Post*, September 20, 1991.

22. *New York Times*, October 10, 1991.

23. *San Diego Times Union*, March 19, 1992.

24. *Columbus Dispatch*, November 2, 1992.

25. *Los Angeles Times*, March 14, 1992.

26. The cohorts are: 1 bounced check (33 members), 2–3 checks (34 members), 4–5 checks (25 members), 6–7 checks (22 members), 8–10 checks (22 members), 11–19 checks (23 members), 20–34 checks (21 members), 35–64 checks (21 members), 65–99 checks (19 members), 100–191 checks (19 members), over 200 checks (27 members).

CHAPTER 5

Biases Without Publicists: Negativity, Race, and Gender Bias in the News

Allegations of partisan bias draw the media, the public, and many academics to the subject. Yet, as we saw in chapter 4, in comparisons of presidents, governors, mayors, and members of Congress, there is no evidence of partisan bias in the media.

That is not to say, of course, that the media are without bias. Three potential forms of bias explored in this chapter, negativity, race, and gender, are significant not just for the effect of slanted news, but also for the lack of ready access for the affected to point out the imbalance.

In short, there are so many members of the two major parties in positions of power that their objections to media coverage are going to be covered and will potentially affect the behavior of the media. In the case of negativity bias, a distinct news preference for negative outcomes over positive, there are no spokespeople for having a positive outlook or trusting politicians in general. For race and gender bias, while there are certainly elected officials in a position to complain about bias, they are in such a distinct minority that they must carefully weigh whether the sliver of media attention they are likely to get should be allocated to complaining about the media or trying to communicate a positive, proactive image to their constituents (See, for example, Zilber and Niven 2000; Niven and Zilber 2001).

Thus, even as there is significant evidence for negativity, race, and gender bias in the media, the attention to these matters pales in comparison to the coverage of partisan bias. Indeed, newspaper attention to partisan bias was greater by a factor of 16 over negativity bias, 23 over racial bias, and 38 over gender bias in 2001.

This chapter revisits the evidence presented in chapter 4, specifically examining the presidential data to explore the effect of negativity, the mayoral data to examine coverage by race, and the congressional data to see whether patterns in coverage are affected by the gender of the subject.

NEGATIVITY

Newspapers across the country report that "too much bad news" is one of the most frequently heard complaints they receive.[1] Indeed, as controversial as the matter of partisan bias has been (at least in academic circles), allegations of a negativity bias in the media go virtually without challenge. That is to say, the prominence and play of negative stories about government and government figures is found to predominate over positive stories in study after study (for example, Diamond, 1978; Fallows 1997; Just et al 1996; Kerbel 1995; Lichter and Noyes 1996; Miller, Goldenberg, and Erbring 1979; Patterson 1994; Robinson and Levy 1985; Sabato 1991).

The Center for Media and Public Affairs finds that Presidents George H.W. Bush and Bill Clinton both received more negative coverage than positive coverage in almost every quarter of every year they served. Smoller (1990) finds that the media are treating successive presidents more negatively and treat individual presidents more negatively as their terms unfold. Presidential campaign coverage has been found not just to dismiss one candidate, but to produce cynical coverage of all of the candidates running for our highest office (Just et al. 1999; Patterson 1994). Concomitantly, Groeling and Kernell (1998) find changes in presidential popularity are more likely to garner media attention when they are in the negative direction than when they are in the positive direction.

While there are professional incentives to avoid the smear of partisan bias allegations, those incentives do not exist with regard to negativity. In contrast to partisan coverage, which will attack the leanings of a large segment of the populace, negative coverage will not upset a general public that is already quite distrustful of politics (for example, Cappella and Jamieson 1996). Moreover, there are no watchdog groups that will immediately serve to point out the unfairness of negative coverage, while there are many that seek to document partisan bias in the news. Finally, negative events are more newsworthy to reporters, who perceive that this is a world where democracy is supposed to work, and that those who serve in our democracy are supposed to be the best (Gans 1980).

Previous studies, however, have not been able to offer conclusions based on comparable results. That is, surely a disaster is more newsworthy than a minor success, but does the media cover minor failures more than minor successes?

PRESIDENTS AND UNEMPLOYMENT: A SECOND LOOK

We saw in the previous chapter that coverage of Bill Clinton and George H.W. Bush was quite similar when their unemployment results were comparable. Another way of examining these data is to consider the relative health or weakness of the economy as a determinant of coverage.

The mean unemployment rate during the period under study was 5.7 percent. Coverage was then matched by comparing articles in months that were equitably spaced above and below that mean (for example, 5.6 percent was compared to 5.8 percent; 4.3 percent to 7.1 percent; and so on).

Table 5.1 shows the amount of coverage in months that were equally above or below the mean. This technique reveals that the higher unemployment months received forty-five percent more coverage, had thirteen percent longer articles, were almost three times as likely to appear on the front page, were almost four times as likely to prominently mention the president, and were decidedly negative in tone toward the president. All these differences are statistically significant at $p < .01$. These data suggest the very real danger for presidents that their good results will garner less attention than their bad, and that the American people will be given a quite misleading picture of their performance.

These indicators were also used in a multivariate analysis that offers us the opportunity to examine whether partisanship and negativity might be subject to effects from each other. An ordinary least squares (OLS) regression model was constructed for each of the five media measures (number of stories, length of stories, page

Table 5.1
Media Coverage of Unemployment When It Is Comparably High or Low

	High	Low
Number of Stories on Unemployment per Month (n=107)	998	551*
Number of words per story (n=4,023)	874	766*
Percent of stories on front page (n=4,023)	8	3*
Percent of stories prominently mention president (n=79,167)	4.3	1.1*
tone of coverage (1=positive, 3=negative) (n=751)	2.7	1.7*

*difference is statistically significant at p < .01, using a 2 tailed t-test.
Note: Based on coverage during the 107 months under study when the unemployment rate was matchable with another month based on having equal distance from the mean. The unit of analysis for the "Number of Stories" measure is the month, for the other variables it is the article.

number of stories, mention of the president, and tone of stories).[2] The independent variables utilized include party (to distinguish between Bush and Clinton), year (to capture changes in media patterns over the time of the study), unemployment rate (which will indicate if the sheer size of the unemployed population drives coverage), change in unemployment rate (which will indicate if increases or decreases in the rate drive coverage), and the absolute value of change in the unemployment rate (which will indicate if change, regardless of which direction, drives coverage).

The results (shown in Table 5.2) reveal that one variable is consistently significant in all five models: the unemployment rate. The higher the unemployment rate, the more coverage given to unemployment, the longer the coverage, the more prominently placed the coverage, the more the president is likely to be prominently mentioned, and the more negative the coverage is likely to be. For every 1 point in the unemployment rate from its low point to its peak, almost 200 more stories are published per month, each of those stories is 70 words longer, over 1 percent more of those stories will focus on the president, each story is 4 pages

Table 5.2

Determinants of Unemployment Coverage Multivariate Regression

	Number of Stories	Prominent mention of President	Number of Words per Article	Page Number of Article	Tone of Article
Unemployment Rate	189.6*	.012*	70.1*	-4.5*	1.4*
Unemployment change	-11.8	-.001	5.2	.4	.07
Unemployment absolute change	105.7*	-.007	27.7	-3.3*	.6
Party	-63.9	-.003	-23.9	-3.1	.24
Year	44.0*	.002	-15.0*	-.2	.14
Constant	-749.7*	-.05*	413.5*	28.2*	-5.2
r^2	.83	.42	.71	.54	.39
n	128	99,430	4971	4971	995

*$p < .01$

Note: Cell entries are unstandardized coefficients. The unit of analysis in the first
   model is the month, in the other four models it is the article.

closer to the front page, and the tone of the story moves a point closer to negative. Given the lack of weight of the "change in unemployment rate," and the inconsistent effect of the "absolute value of change in the unemployment rate," the media do not appear to be reacting to change or improvements in unemployment with nearly as much zeal as they react to a continuing high unemployment rate. The "absolute value of the change in unemployment" does produce more stories (a 1 percent change brings 106 more stories) and more prominent stories (a 1 percent change brings articles 3 pages closer to the front) but does not affect the tone, length, or mentions of the president. As those who accuse the media of a negativity bias might expect, the success of the unemployment rate variable in these models suggests the media react to this issue most often when it is continually bad, and least often when it is continually good.

More to the point, for those who see partisan bias at the heart of media behavior, the party variable was not significant in any of the five models. In short, coverage of unemployment was driven by the total size of the unemployment situation and not the party of the White House occupant.

The final variable in the models, the year, shows that as time passed more stories were being written, but each year saw stories that were slightly shorter.

Figure 5.1
Coverage of Unemployment by Unemployment Rate during Clinton and Bush Administrations

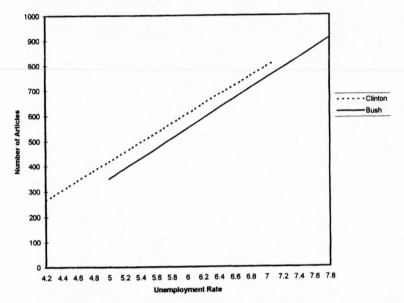

To illustrate the relative weight of party and negativity in determining the number of articles written, Figure 5.1 applies the coefficients for unemployment rate and partisanship while holding all other variables constant. We can see clearly that the number of articles rises dramatically with the unemployment rate. Low unemployment translates to fewer articles for both presidents, while high unemployment translates to more articles for both presidents. That Clinton receives slightly more coverage is likely a modest bonus during the low unemployment periods, but also a modest detriment during the high unemployment periods.

The five models, with explained variance of between .39 and .83, all suggest that party is not a significant factor in unemployment coverage. As was the case in the bivariate comparisons, it is a question of whether unemployment is in relatively good shape or bad that drives coverage on this very important political issue. And bad is decidedly more interesting to the media.

RACE

As is the case for allegations of negativity in the media, complaints about the racial imbalance in coverage generate far less media attention than does concern over partisan bias. Nevertheless, differences in the coverage of African American and white public officials have been highlighted by both African American leaders and scholars (e.g., Grainey, Pollack, and Kusmierek 1984; Gibbons 1993; K. Reeves 1997; Terkildsen and Damore 1999; Payne 1988; Barber and Gandy 1990; Chaudhary 1980; Bell 1973; Zilber and Niven 2000; Clawson and Tom 1999).

Two areas where researchers have found a connection between race and media coverage are the tendency to pay more attention to African Americans when the subject is a negative topic and to credit African American leaders with less effectiveness in their work.

Indeed, African American political leaders are not considered newsworthy on many topics (Gibbons 1993; Clawson and Tom 1999). Byrd (1997, 96), conducting a self-study of the *Washington Post*, found that images of whites in the paper were much more likely to be positive than images of African Americans. Moreover, Entman (1994) finds that it is in negative situations, in which they are lamenting failures, not celebrating victories, that African American leaders will most often be heard on the news.

While political leaders must assert their capacity to get things done, researchers have suggested that the media often write off African Americans, deriding their capacity to accomplish goals or make a contribution (Martindale and Dunlap 1997). Whether the characterization is one of lack of commitment to the work of governing or lack of ability to influence fellow politicians, some argue that the media are prone to question the likelihood of African American success (Broh 1987) or harp on instances of African American failure (Entman 1994).

Importantly, though, previous findings on coverage of African American leaders are based on three methods of study that do not afford opportunities for objective comparison. The first, utilized by researchers such as Gibbons (1993), documents media coverage of African American leaders without any comparison sample. Obviously neither the degree of imbalance, nor even the existence of an imbalance is truly demonstrated without some means of assessing the coverage relative to the treatment of whites.

The second technique compares treatment of African Americans and whites in situations such as campaigns that pit African American and white candidates against each other (Terkildsen and Damore 1999; K. Reeves 1997; Grainey, Pollack, and Kusmierek 1984;

Payne 1988). Such work quite usefully documents the pictures the media paint of the candidates in such campaigns, but cannot directly address the existence of media bias. The candidates in those races can, of course, be quite dramatically different in almost all facets of politics, thus differences in coverage could legitimately flow from those political differences.

The third technique, utilized by Barber and Gandy (1990), studies coverage of African Americans and whites who have been matched on important political characteristics. Barber and Gandy, for example, compare coverage of African Americans in Congress to the coverage received by a matched sample of whites chosen to replicate the length of career and committee service of African American members. While this method is a an improvement over having no means of comparison, it still suffers from an inability to construct truly equivalent comparison samples. A finding of imbalance in coverage relies on the premise that the white and African American politicians should have received similar coverage in the first place. Even if their committees match, there is ample room for differences in priorities, behavior, and success.

Gans (1980), however, offers both an academic and insider's perspective in *Deciding What's News* that suggests racial bias may be prevalent. Gans studied the process of story selection and everything else—from writing to editing—that goes into the articles we see in the news. Gans suggests that reporters are very much trained to deal with the typical and are prone to fit the news into a pre-formed script with which they work. Because of this, conventions develop that may go completely unremarked by reporters, but which powerfully inform their work. For example, reporters are trained to be "objective" in their reporting—thus, a report might balance the comments of a Republican official with the comments of a Democratic official. This is typical, unremarkable, and thought by many to be wonderfully objective. Those who do not fit neatly into the typical political world, however, might not find the process as fair. To wit, news coverage largely excludes the third, fourth, or fifth political parties from virtually any coverage (Herrnson and Faucheux 1999). Similarly, because African American leaders do not fully resemble the typical political actor, they are forced into their own scripts in which they are not half of a typical political dyad, but instead are almost exclusively consulted to offer their perspective about race (Zilber and Niven 2000).

Returning to the research design on coverage of mayors and crime, a group of eight cities (again with populations over 500,000) that have elected an African American and white mayor in the last twenty years were selected. The eight cities are New York, Los Angeles, Chicago, Houston, Dallas, Philadelphia, San Francisco, and Baltimore. Depending on the city, there were between one and three newspapers available for analysis.

Again, all newspapers that were electronically searchable and featured a local section dedicated to city politics were included, although results have been weighted to equalize the importance of each city in the analysis.[3]

Coverage was examined during the period of January 1, 1980 to December 31, 2000. Searching the archives of the newspapers for this period yielded 2,162 articles on the mayor and the city murder rate/murder problem (or other synonymous phrases such as homicide rate). For each of those articles, a team of thirty-one coders determined whether prominent mention was made of the mayor (using mention of the mayor in the headline or first three paragraphs of the story as the standard) and the placement of the article (page number). For a random sample of half of the articles (1,081 articles), coders assessed the portrayal of the effectiveness of the mayor.

All comparisons are made between mayors who produced comparable results. Coverage of mayors for each city in each year has again been sorted into seven groups based on their relative effect on the murder rate (reduced 10 percent or more, reduced 5–9 percent, reduced 1–4 percent, less than 1 percent change, increased 1–4 percent, increased 5–9 percent, increased 10 percent or more) according to FBI statistics.

Unlike the comparison of party, coverage of race and mayors produces notable differences (Table 5.3). African American mayors are subject to more personal attention when the murder rate is increasing than are whites, and less personal attention when the murder rate is decreasing than are whites. For an African American mayor, this means the media help spread the news of your failures while downplaying your connection to successes. In all categories, African Americans were the recipients of less desirable outcome than whites (i.e., less personal prominence in coverage of good outcomes, more prominence in coverage of bad) and in all categories the differences are statistically significant. The placement of the article reveals less severe differences, however. Here,

Table 5.3
Media Coverage of Mayor by Race

	Mayor Prominently Mentioned (n=2162)		Placement of Article (n=2162)		Effectiveness of Mayor (n=1081)	
	AA	WHITE	AA	WHITE	AA	WHITE
Reduced 10% or more	33	39*	2	4*	1.5	1.2+
Reduced 5-9%	24	27*	6	5	1.6	1.3+
Reduced 1-4%	25	22*	8	7	2.1	1.7+
Less than 1% change	10	5*	8	9	2.3	2.1+
Increased 1-4%	22	19*	5	6	2.6	2.5
Increased 5-9%	35	23*	2	4*	2.9	2.7+
Increased 10% or more	38	26*	2	3*	2.9	2.7+

N = 1081
*difference between African American and White total is significant using Chi-Square (p < .05)
+difference between African American and White total is significant using t-test (p < .05)
Note: Mayor prominently mentioned is percentage of all articles in which mayor is mentioned in headline or lead paragraphs; placement of article is the average page number of the articles; Effectiveness of mayor is a three point scale (1 = positive, 2 = neutral, 3 = negative); racial focus is percentage of all articles in which the race of victims, assailants, or the mayor is mentioned.

African Americans saw their coverage closer to the front page for the very worst outcomes, but also closer to the front page for the very best outcomes.

The effectiveness measure, conversely, again reveals dramatic differences. The effectiveness measure shows that not only is the personal attention to the mayor less palatable for African Americans, those same articles will be more harshly critical of African Americans. African Americans who presided over an increasing murder rate received coverage that was seven percent more negative on the three point scale than whites who produced comparable results. At the other end of the spectrum, whites who oversaw a reduction in the murder rate attracted coverage that was ten percent more positive than African Americans who produced comparable results.

These results suggest that mayoral leadership is viewed through colored lenses by the media. The same success that is bigger and brighter for a white mayor is smaller and duller for an African American mayor. Meanwhile, an inability to fix the violent crime problem is a more personal failure for African American mayors than for Whites.

Taken together, twenty-one years of coverage of mayors of both races suggests that African American mayors are subject to a tilted media that holds them to different standards. While the partisan gap was not substantial, the difference between coverage of white and African American members is distinct.

GENDER

In one final reexamination of the data, media coverage of Congressional check bouncers is reconsidered with a comparison between men and women.

That there are differences in coverage between women and men political leaders has been the subject of a number of studies. Scholars have found that women candidates and legislators are taken less seriously (Braden 1996; Witt, Paget, and Matthews 1995; Kahn and Goldenberg 1991; Devitt 1999), receive less coverage (Clawson and Tom 1999), and receive attention on "women's issues" such as abortion and family leave (Carroll and Schreiber 1997) while being ignored on most other matters of substance (Braden 1996; Clawson and Tom 1999). News coverage of women more frequently mentions their family situation and is more likely to invoke matters of the most superficial nature, such as personality, appearance, and fashion decisions (Braden 1996; Witt, Paget, and Matthews 1995; Gidengil and Everitt 1999; Devitt 1999). Men, meanwhile, can expect greater attention to their experience and accomplishments, as well as greater attention to their issue stands (Devitt 1999; Davis 1982; Jamieson 1995).

Not only do male candidates receive more issue coverage, but that issue coverage is more likely to suggest that men are prepared, qualified, and understand the logic and evidence of the issue at hand (Devitt 1999). Ultimately, the portrait of women that emerges from the press suggests that they are simply less pow-

Table 5.4
Coverage of Bounced Checks by Sex

	Men	Women
% stories on checks (n=10,906)	16.1	16.5*
Placement (n=1766)	9.0	8.6*
Length (n=1766)	754	767
Tone (n=833)	2.3	2.5+

*difference is significant at p < .05 using Chi-Square.
+difference is significant at p > .05 using t-test.

erful and less weighty players in the political game (Carroll and Schreiber 1997; Clawson and Tom 1999; Devitt 1999).

Significantly, these beliefs about women politicians commonly advanced by the news media are widely accepted by the American voter (Koch 1999; Alexander and Andersen 1993; Huddy and Terkildsen 1993). Moreover, according to press secretaries to women members of Congress, perceptions that women members are out of the loop, cannot get things done, insubstantial, and interested only in some people's problems are serious concerns that have to be overcome for a woman to maintain a political career (Niven and Zilber 2001). Indeed, Kahn and Goldenberg (1991) argue, and experimental research has shown (Kahn 1992; Dayhoff 1983), that typical media coverage of women candidates can serve to undermine women's credibility with voters.

Taking the same articles previously analyzed for partisan differences in coverage and utilizing the same cohorts of check bouncers reveals an interesting pattern when the results are compared by gender (Table 5.4). Although Democrats and Republicans received quite similar coverage for their comparable check writing indiscretions, men and women did not.

Indeed, in all four categories measured, men receive better treatment, and in three of those categories the differences are statistically significant. Which is to say, men in the House who bounced the same number of checks as women were subject to fewer articles on their banking habits, less prominent placement of those articles, and a less negative tone in those articles.

Could this pattern result from other political factors, such as the members' political standing, experience, or importance in the House? A multivariate regression was constructed using the percentage of stories on bounced checks as a dependent variable. In-

Table 5.5
Determinants of Stories on Bounced Checks Multivariate Regression

	b
Bounced checks	.16**
Party	.01
Race	.02
Sex	.01
Bounced checks x Party	-.008
Bounced checks x Race	.04**
Bounced checks x Sex	.02**
Years in office	-.2
Leadership	1.9
Political Strength	-.1*
Constant	16.8*
R²	.79

N = 266
**p > .01
*p > .05
Note: Cell entries are unstandardized coefficients. Dependent variable is the number of articles written on each member's check bouncing.

dependent variables included the number of bounced checks; party (0 = Republican, 1 = Democrat); sex (0 = man, 1 = woman); an interaction between bounced checks and party; an interaction between bounced checks and sex; years in office; leadership status (1 = party leadership position, committee chair or ranking member, 0 = no); and political strength (margin of victory over opponent in last general election). Given the pattern with regard to coverage of race and mayors, two variables, race (0 = white, 1 = non-white) and an interaction between bounced checks and race, were also added to the model.

Consistent with the bivariate results, the regression shows that party is not a significant factor in the number of bounced check stories, while race and sex are significant (Table 5.5). Combined with the total number of bounced checks and the political strength of the member, the interactions between bounced checks and race and bounced checks and sex are the most meaningful determinants of the number of bounced check stories. To illustrate the regression results, three figures were constructed applying the coefficients to the mean member totals of all variables except the number of bounced checks and the party, race, and sex of the member. The figures are constructed to show the estimated number of stories given 1, 10, or 100 bounced checks.

Figure 5.2
Stories on Bounced Checks: Democrats vs. Republicans

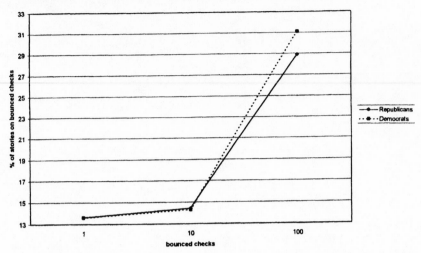

Figure 5.2 suggests that Democrats and Republicans received nearly identical coverage at 1 or 10 bounced checks, with Democrats receiving more coverage than Republicans when each have bounced 100 checks. Meanwhile, comparing men and women shows no difference at 1 check, a slight difference at 10 checks, and more stories on women at 100 checks (Figure 5.3). Similarly, comparing whites and African Americans also shows little difference at one bounced check, but ten produce a few more stories on African Americans, and 100 bounced checks produce a larger gap (Figure 5.4).

Many researchers have asserted that the origin of bias in the media lies in the makeup of the newsroom. As was discussed in chapter 3, Democrats far outnumber Republicans in the media. Moreover, half of all U.S. newspapers have no African American reporters (Campbell 1995), white reporters outnumber African American reporters 8 to 1 (Campbell 1995), and African American newspaper editors are outnumbered by whites 16 to 1 (Gibbons 1993). For women, the imbalance is not as dramatic, but is nevertheless apparent. At the *New York Times*, for example, articles by male authors outnumber articles by female authors by five to one (Mills 1997), while more generally, male reporters outnumber women two to one nationwide (Weaver 1997).

Such imbalances could produce media coverage tinged with the

Figure 5.3
Stories on Bounced Checks: Men vs. Women

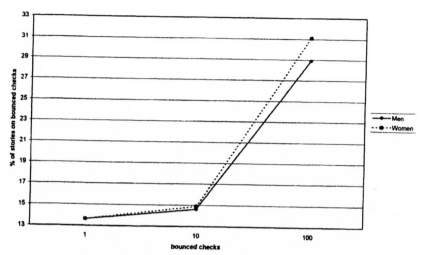

ramifications of the out-group effect. In brief, we tend to identify with, like, better understand, and think more about those who share surface similarities with ourselves (Leach, Peng, and Volckens 2000). Moreover, negative traits of the in-group tend to be explained away as isolated and not indicative of the person's character, while negative traits of the out-group tend to be emphasized and made to represent the person (Gramzow, Gaertner, and Sedikides 2001). This is particularly true in the choice of language to describe the out-group (see Short 2000 for review). If male, white, Democrats do most of the reporting, it is with other male, white, Democrats with whom they will identify (their in-group), and it is those who fall outside of this group who are more likely to be stereotyped based on their surface differences from the reporter and more likely to be reproached for their shortcomings.

Neither the pattern illustrated in chapter 4 nor the results in chapter 5 are consistent with this theory, however. Instead, the combination of partisan balance with a race, gender, and negativity imbalance is consistent with the distribution effect, in which politicians would be judged not in comparison to the reporter, but in comparison to other politicians. Those who have fairly typical traits would be treated as if they belonged in office, while those who have atypical traits would be paid attention to mostly for their differences and shortcomings compared to other officehold-

Figure 5.4
Stories on Bounced Checks: Whites vs. African Americans

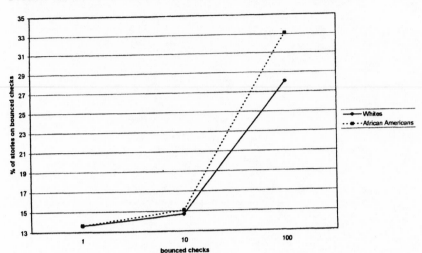

ers (Cejka and Eagly 1999). Given that neither Democrats nor Republicans are rare, they would not be subject to this effect. Women and African Americans, however, who each made up just six percent of the House in 1992, were unusual, and remain unusual in the House.[4] Indeed, the same argument applies to positive and negative outcomes. Researchers have demonstrated that the expectation for positive political results predominates, thus making negative outcomes more notable for their difference (for example, Lau 1985).

CONCLUSION

As consistent as the absence of difference in comparisons of Democrats and Republicans is the presence of differences in coverage of race, gender, and negative outcomes. In situations that are logically equivalent regarding the crime rate for Mayors, whites received better coverage than African Americans. Regarding the bouncing of checks, men received better coverage than women, and regarding the unemployment rate, increases received more coverage than decreases of equal size.

Ultimately, the search for media bias reveals that the brightest lights have been pointed in the wrong direction. That is, attention to allegations of partisan bias is constant despite the thinness of the evidence. Conversely, attention to race, gender, and negativity as forms of bias is paltry even though the evidence is robust.

NOTES

1. *Louisville Courier-Journal*, August 9, 2000; *Los Angeles Times*, December 20, 1999; *Detroit News*, May 3, 2000.

2. The "percent of stories on the front page" variable has been converted to the page number of the article for this analysis.

3. Newspapers utilized include *Daily News, New York Post, New York Times, Los Angeles Times, Chicago Sun-Times, Chicago Daily News, Houston Chronicle, Philadelphia Inquirer, Philadelphia Daily News, Dallas Morning News, Fort Worth Star Telegram, San Francisco Chronicle,* and *Baltimore Sun.*

4. The number of women serving in the House is available from the Center for American Women and Politics fact sheet (www.rci.rutgers.edu/~cawp). The number of African Americans serving in the House is available from the Congressional Black Caucus (www.Congressional BlackCaucus.com). While both groups have experienced gains in the interim, both remain in the decided minority in the House. In 2002, women made up 13.5 percent of the House, and African Americans 8.5 percent.

CHAPTER 6

The Partisans Who Cried Wolf: Implications of the Media Bias Claims, Coverage, and Reality

The results clearly indicate that when they produce comparable outcomes, Democratic and Republican presidents, governors, mayors, and members of Congress receive comparable coverage. There is simply no great disparity in their treatment and no evidence to substantiate charges of partisan bias. This pattern emerges despite a mountain of coverage concerning partisan media bias, a consensus among Americans that the media are untrustworthy and biased, and a scholarly muddle that alternatively finds or disputes claims of bias, but does so without any meaningful baseline from which to study coverage.

THE NEED FOR A BASELINE

Bias cannot be substantiated without a comparison. Coverage, regardless of how unpleasant it may be, cannot be called biased unless there is some mechanism to illustrate that the same coverage is not being proffered to an opposing idea, candidate, or event. Even with a comparison, though, the equality of the situation is crucial. Democrats and Republicans do not always produce the same outcomes, do not always have the same approach, do not always have the same personal skills, and cannot be assumed to inherently deserve equal treatment.

An extreme example illustrates the point. Imagine building the case for media bias by demonstrating the gargantuan differences in media coverage received by Republican President Herbert Hoover and the Democratic challenger who defeated him in 1932, Franklin Roosevelt. Roosevelt was revered internationally for the successes of World War II and the battle against the Depression. Hoover was widely blamed for his perceived political indifference to the economic suffering of the time. Differences in media treatment would emerge in every conceivable comparison—from the campaign trail to coverage of Oval Office decisions. But those differences would represent not a shred of evidence of media bias. For the media to react to reality is not evidence of bias, and, as such, to react to differences between Democrats and Republicans is not evidence of bias.

The evidence offered here is not just another study to be added to the list of findings supporting or undermining claims of bias. Instead, this research offers evidence on media bias that starts with a meaningful and unique baseline from which to compare coverage. At each of the four levels of office in which a comparison is made, it is made between opposite partisans who have produced the same results.

For president, coverage of George H.W. Bush and Bill Clinton is compared during periods when they produced equal unemployment rates. For a group of 100 Democratic and 100 Republican governors, coverage is compared during periods when they produced equal results with regard to their states' unemployment and murder rates. For the Democratic and Republican mayors of eight cities, coverage is compared during periods when they had an equal effect on the murder rate. And finally, for hundreds of Democratic and Republican U.S. House members, coverage is compared during a period when they had bounced a comparable number of checks. In each case, media treatment did not vary by party. In other words, Democrats were neither the beneficiaries nor the victims of any great media bias. Nor were the Republicans.

Despite what can only be called partisan balance in coverage, this equality is not repeated with regard to the matters of negativity, race, and gender.

Taking the unemployment coverage and comparing not the partisan difference, but the positive or negative direction of the situation, reveals that bad news trumps good news in every measure examined. That is, for example, a 1 percent decline in the unemployment rate is less newsworthy than a 1 percent increase in the unemployment rate.

Similarly, coverage of mayors, when compared by race instead of partisanship, revealed significant and consistent differences. We see that mayors with comparable records received coverage that differed markedly on such measures as the prominence of the mayor and the tone of the coverage. This difference repeatedly favors the white mayor, who gets more personal coverage and more positive coverage when results are favorable and less personal coverage and less negative coverage when results are worsening.

And, bounced check for bounced check, even as party does not matter, gender does. For the same indiscretion as their male colleagues, women were treated to both more coverage of the problem and more seriously negative depictions of their actions.

These patterns are important for the effect they are no doubt having on the American people. Researchers have found, evidence, for example, that the negative tenor of the media is decreasing trust in government (Cappella and Jamieson 1996; Graber 1997; Miller, Goldenberg, and Erbring 1979; Robinson 1976; Rozell 1994). Others find that the media coverage typically received by African American leaders is a significant detriment to their securing the support of white voters (Zilber and Niven 2000). Indeed, the contrast is stark, as the more news African American voters consume, the more they like white elected officials, while the more news white voters consume, the less they like African American officials (Zilber and Niven 2000, chapter 5). Meanwhile, the coverage received by women has been linked to the perpetuation of stereotypical assessments of women leaders (Koch 1999).

All this stands in stark contrast to the thrust of both media coverage of itself and public perceptions of the media. Coverage alleging a bias that favors Democrats and liberals is prevalent in the media. Moreover, it is based on a diverse group of sources and often carries with it the weight of definitive sounding evidence. Concomitantly, the American people are more than ready to accept the conclusion that their media sources are biased. Nearly nine in ten believe that reporters use their own political preferences in deciding how to cover events, and a substantial majority believed reporters were rooting for one of the major presidential candidates in the 2000 election.

Meanwhile, academic research can be found to support almost

any perspective on media bias, from liberal bias to conservative bias, to no bias at all. Unfortunately, that evidence lacks a baseline foundation from which to make fair comparisons.

Thus we are left with a media that is besieged with allegations of bias even when it is fair (with regard to partisanship) and all but given a free pass in areas where it is not (that is, on negativity, race, gender). In other words, vast attention and consideration is given to addressing a partisan bias in the media for which there is little evidence. Meanwhile, comparatively little interest is expressed in addressing negativity, race, or gender bias in the media, even as evidence for these patterns grows.

As a number of scholars have warned, our collective interest in media bias is set less in proportion to the seriousness of the problem as it is to the number of complainers. Page and Shapiro (1992) point to near universal media embrace of capitalism, minimal government, and nationalism as examples of media biases that go unremarked because there are few complaining, and even fewer among the observers the media consider notable. Entman (1996, 78) thinks of partisan bias allegations as the great distraction: "Concern with ideological bias has obscured the systematic, consistent biases that the media truly do impose on their narrations of politics and policy."

Gans (1980) and Tuchman (1978) among others have pointed out that the news media tend to parrot the dominant thinking of society. Such a process does not make for a partisan media, since there is no single dominant party. Such as process does not make for a liberal or conservative media, since neither is the philosophy of most Americans. As Dennis (1997, 119) put it, "Partisan viruses are inoculated by the profit motive, by the bottom line in a ferociously competitive business. The media, alas, are centrist, determinedly so." Nevertheless, serving the great American consensus leaves tremendous room for emphasizing the negative in politics, and for treating men and whites as the political norm. Even as these biases may be affecting the American people (Gerbner et al. 1982), we hear less and know less about them. Neither negativity, race, nor gender bias has the equivalent of Senator John McCain calling a news anchor a Trotskyite to dramatize the problem or a phalanx of columnists pointing out, and in some cases, making up, examples of these forms of bias.

THE IMPORTANCE OF ALLEGATIONS

While the prevalence of allegations of partisan bias and the relative absence of allegations regarding negativity, race, and gender bias do nothing to change the reality of the situation, they very powerfully inform perceptions of reality.

Media credibility influences not only how people react to the news (Davis 1990, Zukin 1981), it influences consumption of news (Bennett, Rhine, Flickinger, and Bennett 1999a), and even trust in government (Bennett, Rhine, Flickinger, and Bennett 1999b).

The situation, according to some, is dire. Kohut and Toth (1998, 112) argue that the media have "drawn down the reservoir of support to a level that is dangerous to itself and democratic society." Lichter and Noyes (1996, 271) assert that "everyone loses if political leaders must communicate with citizens via information media that much of the public doesn't trust."

Allegations, whether true or not, matter. And allegations of partisan bias may be undermining trust and use of the media, trust in the government, and in the process, costing Americans one of the few avenues of community left in their lives.

To take a look at this process through the lens of partisan bias allegations, an experiment was conducted in which participants read a newspaper article containing either a realistic depiction of media fairness with regard to partisanship (condition 1), or an article containing a typical depiction of media partisan bias (condition 2), or an article unrelated to the subject (condition 3). The wording of each article is provided in the appendix.

Participants were found in waiting areas of two South Florida airports during May 2001. They were asked if they would be willing to read a brief newspaper article and answer a few questions about it. Of those asked, approximately six in ten agreed to participate. In total, 312 read an article and answered questions. Each was randomly assigned to one of three conditions.

While the respondents are not a representative sample of any larger group, they are a far more diverse group than would be available in any college classroom setting (see Sears 1986). Moreover, this method allows for the use of an experimental design that would otherwise be impractical in a mass-survey format.

After reading the article, participants were asked a number of media trust questions similar to those discussed in chapter 2, and a range of trust and efficacy questions typically used by the National Election Studies.

Given the widespread distrust of the media, it is perhaps not surprising that the experimental manipulation did not have a dramatic effect on media trust. To the question, "Please tell me how you would rate the honesty and ethical standards of people who work as newspaper reporters—very high, high, average, low, or very low?" only 18 percent of those in condition one chose very high or high, with 15 percent of those in conditions two and three choosing that category. Similarly, in response to "How often do you think members of the news media let their own political preferences influence the way they report the news—often, sometimes, seldom, or never?" 85 percent of those in condition one, 88 percent of those in condition three, and 92 percent of those in condition two answered often or sometimes.

There was a somewhat larger difference when participants were asked if the media had treated Al Gore and George W. Bush fairly in the 2000 election coverage. A majority of those in condition one said yes to both (65 percent and 55 percent, respectively), while a majority of those in condition two said no both (49 percent said the media had been fair to Gore, 37 percent said the media had been fair to Bush). In the control group, condition three, 60 percent said the media had been fair to Gore, and 42 percent said the media had been fair to Bush.

The pattern of these results suggests that belief in media bias is so ingrained that the experimental treatment had little effect. In short, it seems that the influence of an article alleging no bias is reduced by the subjects' resistance to a new message, while exposure to an article claiming that there is bias is modest because those beliefs were already present. The similarity in the reaction of these two groups to the control group underscores not only the widespread distrust of the media, but also the depth of that distrust.

Nevertheless, a distinction exists with regard to evaluations of the media overall and evaluations of treatment of individual leaders. When asked to respond to coverage of Al Gore and George W. Bush, the groups were no longer indistinguishable, were overall less distrustful of the media, and showed an inclination to differentiate between Gore and Bush. This suggests the possibility that belief in media bias is built on an amorphous foundation, not directed toward particular instances or coverage of individual leaders, but instead based on generalizations about media outlets, stories, and events.

Most chillingly from the media's perspective, perhaps, are responses to the statement, "Sometimes the media has too much freedom to report what they want." All three groups agreed with the assertion, with those in condition two offering the most support at 75 percent (with those in condition one at 62 percent and in condition three, 68 percent).[1]

In an open-ended question asking for a brief response to the question, "What comes to mind when you think about the news media (television news, newspapers, radio news, etc.)?" responses were also influenced by the bias condition. Those in condition two were more apt to use phrases such as "slanted," "selfish," "self-interested," "They have an agenda," "unfair," and "distorted." Indeed, one respondent filled the available box and then kept writing on the back side of the paper with comments such as: "You think I trust the media? Come on, they're out pushing for their guys all the time. Anyone can see that." While variations of bias complaints appeared in conditions one and three, they were less prevalent. Respondents in condition three were least likely to list multiple bias-related phrases in their comments. Again this suggests that media bias coverage may have so thoroughly poisoned the well that even the condition one article claiming the media were fair triggered some negative thoughts about the media, leaving the media somewhat less offensive to those in condition three, who read about a subject unrelated to media bias.

Interestingly, in a series of questions on trust and efficacy with regard to the federal government, the media-are-biased article (condition two) did tend to increase negative feelings about government. To the question, "How much of the time do you think you can trust the government in Washington to do what is right—just about always, most of the time or only some of the time?" 55 percent of participants in condition one and 58 percent of those in condition three chose the response "only some." In condition two, however, 68 percent chose "only some." Similarly, in response to the question, "Do you think that quite a few of the people running the government are crooked, not very many are, or do you think hardly any of them are crooked?" a minority of conditions one (42 percent) and three (40 percent) chose "quite a few" while a majority of those in condition two (53 percent) chose "quite a few."

Two efficacy questions that tested whether subjects felt the government cared and responded to them produced a basically similar pattern. When asked whether "public officials don't care much what people like me think," 61 percent of those in condition one and 67 percent of those in condition two agreed. Seventy-two percent of those in condition three agreed. As for the assertion, "People like me don't have any say about what the government does," 43 percent of condition one, 49 percent of condition two, and 56 percent of condition three agreed.

While researchers have heretofore found little connection between media use and political participation (Wilkins 2000; Pinkleton, Austin, Fortman 1998), or media use and trust in specific government offices (Moy, Pfau, Kahlor 1999), one must wonder whether this is a pattern that can be sustained in the long term, given the potential for negative views of the media to potentially discourage use of the media, reduce information and interest in elections, and undermine trust and efficacy.

Nevertheless, it is clear that media coverage of media bias has already had a substantial effect. Many of the respondents seemed all but impervious to new information as they had already firmly decided that the media are biased. Despite this pattern, the article that claimed to have evidence of media bias did increase negative feelings for the media and support for the notion that the media have too much freedom. In response to our political system, the media bias article also produced lower trust and efficacy.

Indeed, the results suggest that the media bias debate is one with no winners and many losers in the form of consumers, the media, and public officials.

Domke, Watts, Shah, Fan (1999), however, do point to one potential beneficiary of the media bias conversation. Their work poses the possibility that media bias claims are a strategy of Republican leaders. The authors find that claims of partisan bias are unrelated to the reality of coverage (that is, Republicans are as likely to complain when they are getting relatively bad coverage as when they are getting relatively good coverage). Instead of realistic complaints, the authors suggest that there is a strategic advantage to griping at the media, both in making appeals to sympathetic voters and in attempting to get the media to soften its tone toward Republicans. In fact, some Republican leaders have admitted as much. Rich Bond, former chair of the Republican National Committee, said that crying media bias has "some strategy to it. I'm a coach of a kids' basketball and little league team. If you watch any great coach, what they try to do is 'work the refs.' Maybe the ref will cut you a little slack on the next one."[2]

STEPS TOWARD WINNING BACK TRUST

While eliminating criticism and charges of bias may not be realistic, the media can take steps to rebuild the disintegrating trust in their industry. Here are eleven suggestions for measures that would improve the fairness of their product, or perhaps more importantly, improve the perception of fairness of their product.

Develop consistent standards for identifying speakers.

Either we need to know the party of a political leader or we do not. Media outlets open themselves to criticism by inconsistently pointing out who is a Republican and who is a Democrat, leading to allegations that they mention the party label in negative stories of Republicans and the party label of Democrats in positive stories. Similarly, the use of ideological labels must be made consistent. Individual speakers should be consistently labeled and all sources in the same story should have a consistent standard applied. Far too many stories feature one source with a political label and then other sources without, implying the unlabeled sources are the fair-minded ones. Moreover, it is not difficult to find examples of individuals who appear in the media as conservative activists one day and nonpartisan experts on the next. The consistent use of labels will not only remove the criticism of playing favorites in the use of labels, it will also help to demonstrate the diversity of voices being consulted in a story.

Develop a clear standard for employee political activity.

It is infuriating to readers or viewers of a news product when they find that journalists have been participating in political events they are supposed to be objectively covering. Kurtz (1994) notes that media outlets ranging from the most prominent (The *New York Times*, The *Washington Post*) to the obscure (The *Fairfield Ledger*) have investigated and ultimately forbidden the political activity of reporters, activity that took place outside the office and on the reporters' own time. Editors of The *Washington Post* warned all their reporters (even those who exclusively cover nonpolitical fare such as sports) that political advocacy on their own time was "unprofessional," and that foregoing the right to political expression "is the choice we make when we choose to work in this business" (quoted in Kurtz, 1994, 148). But, as Fallows (1997) notes, even these kinds of standards overlook the numerous opportunities prominent reporters have to give lucrative speeches to corporations and wealthy interest groups. In the process, these reporters tend to expose themselves to people with a very distinct political perspective and walk away with a fresh sympathy for their special interest. Thus, standards of outside political activity must cover not just the overt political acts one might immediately think of, but any action that would tend to indicate bias, or create bias, on the part of the journalist.

Develop more clear standards of newsworthiness.

Newspapers across the country have standing policies regarding the coverage of sports teams. The most significant area team warrants multiple reporters for both home and away games. Less important local teams might get multiple reporters for home games and a single reporter for away games. Minor teams might be assigned one reporter for home games and no reporters for away games. The logic of the assignment of manpower is clear and consistent. An editor considers the resources available, the importance of the subject, and creates a standard that is openly applied. Readers, writers, even the teams, know when they should expect coverage and when they should not. Despite the greater importance of politics, standards of coverage appear far more haphazard.

Indeed, if there is any standard applied in covering candidates, it seems to revolve around standing in the polls (Patterson 1994). Such a standard makes for a self-fulfilling prophesy of media coverage: those who are ahead in the polls get coverage. Without coverage other candidates cannot gain in the polls, and thus those who are ahead in the polls tend to stay ahead in the polls.[3] This creates a closed process based not on qualifications or quality of ideas but on the arbitrary starting point of candidates in the polls. Indeed, Patterson (1994) suggests that one of the first things voters learn about the leading candidate in the polls is that he is the leading presidential candidate in the polls. Instead, the media should utilize a standard that affords coverage more consistently and more rationally. For example, on the presidential level, candidates on the ballot in enough states to win the presidency should be covered, regardless of their standing in the polls. Such a standard, logically created and known in advance, would provide the media, the voters, and the candidates with some security that newsworthiness had been decided on a fair basis.

Results should be audited.

Crack open the annual report for the *New York Times* company and you will see a striking contrast between the way the company establishes that they have succeeded in fulfilling their fundamental goals, which the company labels "core values." For the goal "creation of long-term shareholder value," the company includes a detailed and audited set of figures, providing profits and expenses for the seventeen newspapers, eight television stations, various magazines, and other subsidiaries the company owns. For their other main goal, providing "content of the highest quality and integrity," the company includes no evidence whatsoever. There are no figures, charts, displays, and certainly no outside verification that the company has approached fairness, quality, or integrity in their coverage. Thus, for the sake of public trust, as well as for the lessons they may learn from the experience, media companies should consider creating a nonpartisan external audit of their coverage.

Every media outlet should have an ombudsperson.

While many newspapers do have a person who functions as an advocate of the readers, every newspaper and every television news team should have such a person. People need to have an outlet to voice their concerns and to receive some kind of response. Moreover, news organizations need to have someone who can thoughtfully examine their operations without responding defensively to every criticism.

Cover more politics in the words of the speaker.

Inherent in the process of reducing our political leaders' comments into five to eight second sound bites is a tremendous shift of power from the speaker to the reporter. Television news has long been criticized for this process, but newspapers are generally just as guilty of this practice. No media outlet is inclined to report entire speeches, but more discretion can still be given to the speaker. For example, some newspapers run articles on political issues by giving opposing candidates a specified space to comment on the issue, and some televisions stations are giving candidates a set number of minutes to make comments on a nightly basis before an election. By doing this, even without a tremendous allocation of space, media outlets are inoculating themselves against charges of bias, while providing access to political leaders consumers would not otherwise enjoy.

Cultivate expertise among reporters.

One reason media outlets can fall prey to the appearance of bias is that reporters may lack the information necessary to be, or to appear to be, fair. For example, coverage of the 2000 presidential recount was often provided by reporters who had no previous experience with a recount of any kind, even in a city council race. As a consequence, reports on the recount process often portrayed the laws, the actors involved, and the likely outcome unrealistically. Such coverage inspired outcries of bias from both sides, as inconsistencies in the coverage provided by various media outlets suggested bias must be influencing coverage.

Have clear and consistent standards regarding reliability of information.

As Kovach and Rosenstiel (1999) point out in their book *Warp Speed*, all too many media outlets have fuzzy standards regarding the reporting of rumors and unverified information. Those standards become even less clear when newspapers and televisions stations report the findings of another media outlet, in effect suspending all in-house standards and relying on the hope that the unknown standards of the source are sufficient. Instead, media outlets should have, and should share, their basic standards. When are anonymous sources appropriate? Is second-hand, third-hand, or fourth-hand information useable?

Create regular occasions for reflection on work.

Given the deadlines that are a constant factor in their work, reporters are often left to finish one story and then begin the next. There are few opportunities to question assumptions, perspectives, or the bigger picture into which their coverage has fit. As Gans (1980) has argued, without some opportunity to scrutinize their work and the context in which they think, journalists are unlikely to improve on or adapt to changing realities or ill-considered assumptions. As an occasional assignment, journalists should be asked to scrutinize their own work and consider the patterns they find in it, both positive and negative.

Perform a public service.

Members of Congress have long known that by tracking down the occasional wayward Social Security check or setting up a shuttle bus to the local Veterans' hospital, there are votes to be won.

People appreciate help provided by someone in a position to get things done. Media outlets are in a position to help people, whether by tracking down information or by raising public and, ultimately, political-leader awareness of a problem. News outlets stand to gain directly and indirectly by staking a claim to their communities' problems. While some newspapers have "ask the expert" columns, and some television stations have consumer investigation reporters, few media outlets have an integrated strategy for being public advocates for the people.

Cover bias skeptically.

Finally, one must note that the media are hard at work undermining confidence in their own institutions. As long as coverage of media bias continues without logic, reason, or evidence, the media will be further eroding confidence in their product regardless of any of these reform ideas they might pursue.

In some ways, of course, complaining about the media is akin to complaining about the weather. Regardless of the conditions, carping will continue because the target is obvious and easy to attack.

But while the weather never listens and the people seldom act on those complaints, dismay with the media is a very real force in our society and in our politics.

NOTES

1. Salwen (1998) has noted that support for censorship is strongly tied to belief in media influence.

2. *New York Times*, August 18, 1992.

3. Perhaps the worst example of the media's candidate newsworthiness standard is the case of Larry Agran. Agran, former mayor of Irvine, California, entered the New Hampshire presidential primary, seeking the Democratic nomination for president in 1992. Agran, considered a minor candidate by the media, struggled to receive any coverage of his candidacy as he competed for attention with Bill Clinton, Paul Tsongas, Tom Harkin, Bob Kerrey, Jerry Brown, and the like. When he was invited to candidate debates with the major contenders, Agran found himself left out of the news coverage and cropped out of the photos. Despite the difficulties, Agran persevered in a retail politics, person to person campaign. Finally, he pledged to the New Hampshire voters that he would be ahead of a major contender in the next statewide poll. Agran, true to his word, surpassed Jerry Brown in a statewide survey, and waited for

the media to confer on him a new status. Instead, media outlets, including ABC News, reported the survey by saying Brown was last among major contenders, and completely deleting Agran from the survey results. Agran's campaign efforts were devastated.

Postscript: Bias and Terror

The events of September 11, 2001, and the subsequent war effort may seem to call into question the significance of the charges, counter charges, and even the evidence, regarding media bias. But in truth, the media become even more important in times of crisis—ratings for cable news networks, for example, more than tripled in the aftermath of September 11—and our trust or distrust of our sources of information thus becomes even more important.

In fact, as a convenient and obvious presence in our lives, world events may have served to underscore the fervor with which the media were criticized. ABC News anchor Peter Jennings was one of the first, and most prominent recipients, of scorn. Or as the *Milwaukee Journal Sentinel* put it, Jennings was tarred by one of the "biggest whoppers out there."[1]

As the *Washington Post* reported, Jennings' office phone line was rendered inoperable with a flood of angry calls in the days after the attack.[2] An ABC News executive described Jennings' voice mail as being filled to capacity with "vitriol, really awful stuff."

What precipitated the outcry against Jennings was a report spread by conservative radio talk show host Rush Limbaugh. Limbaugh announced that Jennings, "this fine son of Canada" had insulted President George W. Bush during the network's coverage of the events of September 11. Limbaugh said, "Little Peter couldn't understand why George Bush didn't address the nation sooner than he did, and even made snide comments like, 'Well, some presidents are just better at it than others,' and 'Maybe it's wise that certain presidents just not try to address the people of the country.' "

Limbaugh ridiculed Jennings' behavior as just another example of "foolish, whining, babyish, unrealistic selfishness on the part of liberals."

Were Limbaugh's criticisms warranted? No. In fact, the misrepresentation of Jennings' words was so severe that the conservative Media Research Center stepped into the fray, and announced that Jennings' alleged comments were either "never uttered, distorted or taken out of context." The group reported that their "analysts reviewed tapes of the entire awful day and found no insults or disrespectful comments by the ABC anchor."[3]

In contrast to Limbaugh's allegations, Jennings had not questioned why the president was kept out of Washington. He said on the air that the Secret Service would take the task of protecting the president's safety with "profound seriousness" and never suggested they should do anything but follow safety imperatives. Jennings also never suggested Bush should avoid addressing the American people, and never implied Bush would be incapable of the task.

The conflict between his charges against Jennings and the reality was so great that even Limbaugh ultimately relented. Limbaugh corrected himself on Jennings, he said, to avoid any "unnecessary angst on the part of our colleagues at ABC."[4] Understandably, Jennings was reported to be "disappointed when people who aren't watching the broadcast assume he said things he didn't say."[5]

Another prime media target has been CNN. The network was accused repeatedly of not using the word *terrorist* to describe those who hijacked planes and attacked the World Trade Center and the Pentagon. Michael Kinsley, writing in the *Washington Post*, called the decision of the network "perverse" and "idiotic."[6] Kinsley's diatribe against CNN was then picked up by other writers, including syndicated columnist Thomas Sowell. Sowell wrote that the network's decision was akin to giving Adolph Hitler equal time to offer his perspective to the American people during World War II.[7]

There is at least one notable hole in Kinsley's and Sowell's indictment of CNN. It simply is not true. A CNN vice president wrote The *Washington Post*, calling Kinsley's assertion "unaccountably inaccurate." Indeed, "for the record, CNN has, since the morning of Sept. 11, called those responsible for the attacks exactly what they are, terrorists."[8] Other journalists who have actually scrutinized CNN's reporting found that the words terrorist, terrorism, and terror are in constant use in CNN's on air coverage and on its news web site.[9]

Both examples underscore the strange reality in which the media are criticized for slanted perspectives by critics whose perspectives are so absurdly tilted that they cannot even pause to consider the veracity of their information before they begin their mantra of calling the media perverse, idiotic, and un-American. To be sure, the media are at times criticized for legitimate failings and shortcomings, but all too often, the media are castigated for things that not only did not occur, but would be as repulsive and inappropriate to the media as they are in the imaginations of their accusers.

The ceaseless, and too often baseless, criticisms of the media serve no real purpose. The ubiquity of the complaints makes it hard, if not impossible, to distinguish between the important and the trivial, the true and the fictional. We have produced a media that cannot possibly respond or improve in the face of endless complaints, and a general public left in the frustrating hold of a media they can neither "fix" nor see much of the world without.

Charges of media bias simply continue to fly—without evidence, without logic, and even without parameters of common sense. It too often seems that the standard for spreading an accusation of media bias represents an inversion of an American principle, as the media are guilty until proven innocent.

NOTES

1. Cuprisin, Tim. 2001. "Terrorism Could Change Television Viewership." *Milwaukee Journal Sentinel*, September 24.

2. Kurtz, Howard. 2001. "Peter Jennings, in the News for What He Didn't Say." *Washington Post*, September 24.

3. Cuprisin, Tim. 2001. "Terrorism Could Change Television Viewership." *Milwaukee Journal Sentinel*, September 24.

4. Kurtz, Howard. 2001. "Peter Jennings, In the News for What He Didn't Say." *Washington Post*, September 24.

5. Ryan, Suzanne. 2001. "Jennings Misquoted." *Boston Globe*, September 25.

6. Kinsley, Michael. 2001. "Defining Terrorism; It's Essential. It's Also Impossible." *Washington Post*, October 5.

7. Sowell, Thomas. 2001. "Loose-lipped Look at One Privilege as a Right." *Sun-Sentinel*, October 15.

8. Binford, Susan. 2001. "CNN on Terrorists." *Washington Post*, October 11.

9. Scheiber, Dave. 2001. "When a Word Fuels the Fear." *St. Petersburg Times*, October 15; Cuprisin, Tim. 2001. "Inside TV & Radio." *Milwaukee Journal Sentinel*, October 1.

Appendix

CONDITION 1

New Study Finds the Media Are Fair to Democrats and Republicans

"There is almost no detectable difference in the treatment of Democrats and Republicans" says a report issued today by a bipartisan commission studying the media. Comparing coverage of unemployment in the United States, the Committee for Media Fairness study finds that Presidents George Bush and Bill Clinton received nearly identical coverage.

Lead study author Bill Wilson says the committee compared eleven years of economic coverage (1989–1999) in 150 newspapers from across the country.

Wilson says the key to this study is that it uses an objective comparison. "In this study, every comparison is based on coverage during periods when the Bush and Clinton administrations produced the same result. We looked at coverage of unemployment, for example, when it was 5.5 percent for Bush, and 5.5 percent for Clinton. If they produced the same results, logically they should get the same coverage. If there is media bias, coverage should be better for one than the other. If there is no bias, coverage should look the same."

The committee found that on such indicators as the number, length, and placement of articles, whether the president was prominently mentioned in the articles, and the tone of the articles when Clinton and Bush produced equal results, they received equal treatment from the media.

The research was funded by a grant from the nonpartisan American Political Science Association.

Wilson believes people will take his group's findings seriously when considering whether the media are biased. "Thoughts about media bias have been a lot like Justice Potter Stewart's definition of pornography, we know it when we see it." Wilson said. "And when you define it, and look for it, you won't see it because it isn't there."

CONDITION 2

New Study Finds the Media Are Biased

"There are almost no similarities in the media's treatment of Democrats and Republicans" says a report issued today by a bipartisan commission. Comparing coverage of unemployment in the United States, the Committee for Media Fairness study finds that Presidents George Bush and Bill Clinton received quite different treatment from the media.

Lead study author Bill Wilson says the committee compared eleven years of economic coverage (1989–1999) in 150 newspapers from across the country.

Wilson says the key to this study is that it uses an objective comparison. "In this study, every comparison is based on coverage during periods when the Bush and Clinton administrations produced the same result. We looked at coverage of unemployment, for example, when it was 5.5 percent for Bush, and 5.5 percent for Clinton. If they produced the same results, logically they should get the same coverage. If there is media bias, coverage should be better for one than the other. If there is no bias, coverage should look the same."

The committee found that on such indicators as the number, length, and placement of articles, whether the president was prominently mentioned in the articles, and tone of the articles, Clinton consistently received better coverage than Bush.

The research was funded by a grant from the nonpartisan American Political Science Association.

Wilson believes people will take his group's findings seriously when considering whether the media are biased. "Thoughts about media bias have been a lot like Justice Potter Stewart's definition of pornography, we know it when we see it," Wilson said. "And when you define it, and look for it, you'll see it because it's there."

CONDITION 3

Renovations for Nation's Busiest Airports

Across the United States, government and airline officials are spending tens of billions of dollars on airport expansions and improvements. Some of these projects are aimed at increasing traffic and reducing the delays that afflicted so many passengers last year—the tardiest year in U.S. air travel history.

Officials at Miami International Airport (33.9 million passengers in 1999) report no major disruptions for travelers. But anyone passing through is likely to encounter signs, inside and outside, of a major expansion.

In all, $5.4 billion in construction is planned, and the work, which began in 1993, is expected to continue through 2008. When it's done, the airport's terminal and radiating concourses will have increased from 4.7 million square feet to 7.4 million.

Additional improvements are scheduled for roadways and parking, along with added space for cargo storage and handling and the addition of a fourth runway. Construction of the new runway, which isn't expected to affect traffic on other runways, is due to be completed in July 2003.

Information officer Inson Kim of the Miami-Dade Aviation Department noted that minor roadwork has been in progress around the airport, but that passengers should find no dramatic changes in the facility's workings.

The airport now features eight concourses, labeled A through H, radiating like fingers from a main terminal. The expansion will eventually connect concourses A-D directly to each other, making a single superconcourse of 47 gates. A new concourse (labeled J, so that travelers don't confuse I with 1) is also planned.

"It's like building a new airport on top of an existing airport," said Kim.

Bibliography

Alexander, D., and Andersen, K. 1993. "Gender as a Factor in the Attribution of Leadership Traits." *Political Research Quarterly* 46: 527–545.

Alford, J., Teeters, H., Ward, D., and Wilson, R. 1994. "Overdraft: The Political Cost of Congressional Malfeasance." *Journal of Politics* 56: 788–801.

Alger, D. 1996. *The Media and Politics*. Belmont, CA: Wadsworth.

Althaus, S., and Tewksbury, D. 2000. "Patterns of Internet and Traditional News Media Use in a Networked Community." *Political Communication* 17: 21–45.

Anju, S., Beavers, S., Berreau, C., Dodson, A., Hibbing, J., Hourigan, P., Showalter, S., and Walz, J. 1994. "Modern Congressional Election Theory Meets the 1992 House Elections." *Political Research Quarterly* 47: 909–922.

Atkeson, L.R., and Partin, R. 1995. "Economic and Referendum Voting: A Comparison of Gubernatorial and Senatorial Elections." *American Political Science Review* 89: 99–107.

Barber, J., and Gandy, O. 1990. "Press Portrayal of African American and White United States Representatives." *Howard Journal of Communications* 2: 213–225.

Barker, D. 1998. "Rush to Action: Political Talk Radio and Health Care Unreform." *Political Communication* 15: 83–97.

Barker, D. 1999. "Rushed Decisions: Political Talk Radio and Vote Choice, 1994–1996." *Journal of Politics* 61: 527–539.

Batlin, R. 1954. "San Francisco Newspapers' Campaign Coverage: 1896, 1952." *Journalism Quarterly* 31: 297–303.

Becker, L., Cobbey, R., and Sobowale, I. 1978. "Public Support for the Press." *Journalism Quarterly* 55: 421–430.

Bell, L.S. 1973. "The Role and Performance of Black and Metro Newspapers in Relation to Political Campaigns in Selected Racially Mixed Congressional Elections." Ph.D. dissertation, Northwestern University.

Bennett, S., Rhine, S., and Flickinger, R. 2001. "Assessing Americans' Opinions about the News Media's Fairness in 1996 and 1998." *Political Communication* 18: 163–182.

Bennett, S., Rhine, S., Flickinger, R., and Bennett, L. 1999a. "Americans' Interest in the News, 1989–1998." Presented at the Annual Meeting of the Southern Political Science Association.

Bennett, S., Rhine, S., Flickinger, R., and Bennett, L. 1999b. " 'Video-malaise' Revisited: Public Trust in the Media and Government." *Harvard International Journal of Press/Politics* 4: 8–23.

Bennett, W.L. 1990. "Toward a Theory of Press-State Relations in the United States." *Journal of Communication* 40: 103–125.

Berelson, B., Lazarsfeld, P., and McPhee, W. 1954. *Voting: A Study of Opinion Formation in a Presidential Campaign*. Chicago: University of Chicago Press.

Bernstein, C., and Woodward, B. 1974. *All the President's Men*. New York: Simon and Shuster.

Beyle, T., Ostdiek, D., and Lynch, G.P. 1996. "Is the State Press Corp Biased?" *Spectrum: The Journal of State Government* 69: 6–16.

Bloom, H.S., and Price, H.D. 1975. "Voter Response to Short-run Economic Conditions: The Asymmetric Effect of Prosperity and Recession." *American Political Science Review* 69: 1240–1254.

Blumberg, N. 1954. *One Party Press?* Lincoln: University of Nebraska.

Bozell, L.B., and Baker, B. 1990. *And That's the Way It Isn't*. Alexandria, VA: Media Research Center.

Braden, M. 1996. *Women Politicians and the Media*. Lexington: University Press of Kentucky.

Broh, C.A. 1987. *A Horse of a Different Color: Television's Treatment of Jesse Jackson's 1984 Presidential Campaign*. Washington, DC: Joint Center for Political Studies.

Buchanan, B. 1991. *Electing a President: The Markle Commission Research on Campaign '88*. Austin: University of Texas Press.

Buell, E. 1987. " 'Locals' and 'Cosmopolitans': National, Regional, and State Newspaper Coverage of the New Hampshire Primary." In *Media and Momentum*, G. Orren and N. Polsby (eds.). Chatham, NJ: Chatham House.

Byrd, J. 1997. "Blacks, Whites in News Pictures." In *Facing Difference: Race, Gender, and Mass Media*, S. Biagi and M. Kern-Foxworth (eds.). Thousand Oaks, CA: Pine Forge Press.

Campbell, C. 1995. *Race, Myth and the News*. Thousand Oaks, CA: Sage.

Cappella, J., and Jamieson, K.H. 1996. "News Frames, Political Cynicism, and Media Cynicism." *The Annals of the American Academy of Political and Social Science* 546: 71–84.

Cappella, J., and Jamieson, K.H. 1997. *Spiral of Cynicism: The Press and the Public Good*. New York: Oxford University Press.

Carroll, S., and Schreiber, R. 1997. "Media Coverage of Women in the 103rd Congress." In *Women, Media, and Politics*, P. Norris (ed.). New York: Oxford University Press.

Carsey, T., and Wright, G. 1998. "State and National Factors in Gubernatorial and Senatorial Elections." *American Journal of Political Science* 42: 991–1002.

Cavanaugh, J. 1995. *Media Effects on Voters: A Panel Study of the 1992 Presidential Election*. Lanham, MD: University Press of America.

Cejka, M., and Eagly, A. 1999. "Gender-stereotypic Images of Occupations Correspond to the Sex Segregation of Employment." *Personality & Social Psychology Bulletin* 25(4): 413–423.

Center for Media and Public Affairs. 1988. "Bad News is Good News for Bush." *Media Monitor* 2.

Center for Media and Public Affairs. 1992. "Clinton's the One." *Media Monitor* 6.

Center for Media and Public Affairs. 1996. "Campaign '96 Final: How TV News Covered the General Election." *Media Monitor* 10.

Chaudhary, A. 1980. "Press Portrayal of Black Officials." *Journalism Quarterly* 57: 636–646.

Cirino, R. 1971. *Don't Blame the People*. New York: Random House.

Clancey, M., and Robinson, M. 1985. "The Media in Campaign '84: General Election Coverage." *Public Opinion* 8: 49–54.

Clarke, H., Feigert, F., Seldon, B., and Stewart, M. 1999. "More Time With My Money: Leaving the House and Going Home in 1992 and 1994." *Political Research Quarterly* 52: 67–85.

Clarke, P., and Evans, S. 1983. *Covering Campaigns: Journalism in Congressional Elections*. Stanford, CA: Stanford University Press.

Clawson, R., and Tom, R. 1999. "Media Coverage of State Legislators: Is There a Gender Bias?" Presented at the Annual Meeting of the Midwest Political Science Association.

Coffey, P. 1975. "A Quantitative Measure of Bias in Reporting of Political News." *Journalism Quarterly* 52(3): 551–553.

D'Alessio, D., and Allen, M. 2000. "Media Bias in Presidential Elections: A Meta-Analysis." *Journal of Communication* 50: 133–156.

Dalton, R., Beck, P., and Huckfeldt, R. 1998. "Partisan Cues and the Media: Information Flows in the 1992 Presidential Election." *American Political Science Review* 92: 111–126.

Danielson, W., and Adams, J. 1961. "Completeness of Press Coverage of the 1960 Campaign." *Journalism Quarterly* 38: 441–452.

Dautrich, K., and Hartley, T. 1999. *How the News Media Fail American Voters: Causes, Consequences, and Remedies.* New York: Columbia University Press.

Davis, D. 1990. "News and Politics." In *New Directions in Political Communication: A Resource Book*, D. Swanson and D. Nimmo (eds.). Newbury Park, CA: Sage.

Davis, J. 1982. "Sexist Bias in Eight Newspapers." *Journalism Quarterly* 59: 456–460.

Dayhoff, S. 1983. "Sexist Language and Person Perception: Evaluation of Candidates from Newspaper Articles." *Sex Roles* 9: 527–539.

Dennis, E. 1997. "How Liberal Are the Media Anyway?" *Harvard International Journal of Press/Politics* 2: 115–119.

Devitt, J. 1999. "Framing Gender on the Campaign Trail: Women's Executive Leadership and the Press." Report for the Women's Leadership Fund.

Diamond, E. 1978. *Good News, Bad News.* Cambridge, MA: MIT Press.

Dickson, S. 1994. "Understanding Media Bias: The Press and the U.S. Invasion of Panama." *Journalism Quarterly* 71: 809–819.

Doll, H., and Bradley, B. 1974. "A Study of the Objectivity of Television News Reporting of the 1972 Presidential Campaign." *Central States Speech Journal* 25: 254–263.

Domke, D., Fan, D., Fibison, M., Shah, D., Smith, S., and Watts, M. 1997. "News Media, Candidates and Issues, and Public Opinion in the 1996 Presidential Campaign." *Journalism and Mass Communication Quarterly* 74: 718–737.

Domke, D., Watts, M., Shah, D., and Fan, D. 1999. "The Politics of Conservative Elites and the 'Liberal Media' Argument." *Journal of Communication* 49: 35–58.

Efron, E. 1971. *The News Twisters.* Los Angeles: Nash.

Einseidel, E., and Bibbee, M. 1979. "The Newsmagazines and Minority Candidates—Campaign '76." *Journalism Quarterly* 56: 102–105.

Entman, R. 1989. *Democracy Without Citizens: Media and the Decay of American Politics.* New York: Oxford University Press.

Entman, R. 1994. "Representation and Reality in the Portrayal of Blacks on Network Television News." *Journalism Quarterly* 71: 509–520.

Entman, R. 1996. "Reporting Environmental Policy Debate: The Real Media Bias." *Harvard International Journal of Press/Politics* 1: 77–92.

Entman, R., and Paletz, D. 1980. "Media and the Conservative Myth." *Journal of Communication* 30: 154–166.

Epstein, E. 1973. *News from Nowhere*. New York: Random House.

Erskine, H. 1970. "The Polls: Opinion of the News Media." *Public Opinion Quarterly* 34: 630–643.

Evarts, D., and Stempel, G. 1974. "Coverage of the 1972 Campaign by TV, Newsmagazines, and Major Newspapers." *Journalism Quarterly* 51: 645–649, 676.

Eveland, W., and Scheufele, D. 2000. "Connecting News Media Use With Gaps in Knowledge and Participation." *Political Communication* 17: 215–237.

Fallows, J. 1997. *Breaking the News*. New York: Vintage.

Fan, D. 1996. "Predictions of the Bush-Clinton-Perot Presidential Race from the Press." *Political Analysis* 6: 67–105.

Fitzsimon, M., and McGill, L. 1995. "The Citizen as Media Critic." *Media Studies Journal* 9: 91–101.

Frank, R. 1973. *Message Dimensions of Television News*. Lexington, MA: Lexington Books.

Friedman, H., Mertz, T, and DiMatteo, M. 1980. "Perceived Bias in the Facial Expressions of Television News Broadcasters." *Journal of Communication* 30: 103–111.

The Gallup Poll. 1986–1999. Wilmington, DE: Scholarly Resources.

Gamson, W., Croteau, D., Hoynes, W., and Sasson, T. 1992. "Media Images and the Social Construction of Reality." *Annual Review of Sociology* 18: 373–393.

Gans, H. 1980. *Deciding What's News*. New York: Vintage.

Gans, H. 1985. "Are U.S. Journalists Dangerously Liberal?" *Columbia Journalism Review* 24(6): 29–33.

Gaziano, C. 1988. "How Credible is the Credibility Crisis?" *Journalism Quarterly* 65: 267–278.

Gaziano, C., and McGrath, K. 1986. "Measuring the Concept of Credibility." *Journalism Quarterly* 63: 451–462.

Gerbner, G., Gross, L., Morgan, M., and Signorielli, N. 1982. "Charting the Mainstream: Television's Contributions to Political Orientations." *Journal of Communication* 32: 100–127.

Gibbons, A. 1993. *Race, Politics, and the White Media: The Jesse Jackson Campaigns*. Lanham, MD: University Press of America.

Gidengil, E., and Everitt, J. 1999. "Metaphors and Misrepresentation: Gendered Mediation in News Coverage of the 1993 Canadian Leaders' Debates." *Harvard International Journal of Press/Politics* 4: 48–65.

Graber, D. 1971. "Press Coverage Patterns of Campaign News: The 1968 Presidential Race." *Journalism Quarterly* 48: 502–512.

Graber, D. 1976. "Effect of Incumbency on Coverage Patterns in 1972 Presidential Campaign." *Journalism Quarterly* 53: 499–508.

Graber, D. 1997. *Mass Media and American Politics*. Washington, DC: Congressional Quarterly Press.

Grainey, T., Pollack, D., and Kusmierek, L. 1984. "How Three Chicago Newspapers Covered the Washington-Epton Campaign." *Journalism Quarterly* 61: 352–363.

Gramzow, R., Gaertner, L., and Sedikides, C. 2001. "Memory for Ingroup and Out-group Information in a Minimal Group Context: The Self as an Informational Base." *Journal of Personality & Social Psychology* 80: 88–205.

Groeling, T., and Kernell, S. 1998. "Is Network News Coverage of the President Biased?" *Journal of Politics* 60: 1063–1087.

Groseclose, T., and Krehbiel, K. 1994. "Golden Parachutes, Rubber Checks, and Strategic Retirements from the 102nd House." *American Journal of Political Science* 38: 75–99.

Gunther, A. 1988. "Attitude Extremity and Trust in the Media." *Journalism Quarterly* 65: 279–287.

Gunther, A. 1992. "Biased Press or Biased Public? Attitudes Towards Media Coverage of Social Groups." *Public Opinion Quarterly* 56: 147–167.

Gunther, A. 1998. "The Persuasive Press Influence: Effects of Mass Media on Perceived Public Opinion." *Communication Research* 25(5): 486–504.

Hale, J. 1993. "Shaping the Conventional Wisdom." *Political Communication* 10: 285–302.

Haynes, A., and Murray, S. 1998. "Why Do the News Media Cover Certain Candidates More than Others? The Antecedents of State and National News Coverage in the 1992 Presidential Nomination Campaign." *American Politics Quarterly* 26: 420–438.

Herrnson, P., and Faucheux, R. 1999. "Outside Looking In: View of Third Party and Independent Candidates." *Campaigns and Elections* 20: 27.

Hertsgaard, M. 1988. *On Bended Knee: The Press and the Reagan Presidency*. New York: Farrar, Straus, and Giroux.

Hess, S. 1981. *Washington Reporters*. Washington, DC: Brookings.

Hewitt, C. 1996. "Estimating the Number of Homeless: Media Misrepresentation of an Urban Problem." *Journal of Urban Affairs* 18: 431–447.

Higbie, C. 1954. "Wisconsin Dailies in the 1952 Campaign: Space vs. Display." *Journalism Quarterly* 31: 56–61.

Hofstetter, C.R. 1976. *Bias in the News: Network Television Coverage of the 1972 Campaign*. Columbus: Ohio State University Press.

Hofstetter, C.R. 1978. "News Bias in 1972: A Cross-Media Comparison."
    Journalism Monographs 58.
Hofstetter, C.R. 1998. "Political Talk Radio, Situational Involvement, and
    Political Mobilization." *Social Science Quarterly* 79: 273–286.
Hofstetter, C.R., and Zukin, C. 1979. "TV Network News and Advertis-
    ing in the Nixon and McGovern Campaigns." *Journalism Quarterly*
    56: 106–115, 152.
Holtgraves, T., and Grayer, A. 1994. " 'I am Not a Crook': Effects of
    Denials on Perceptions of a Defendant's Guilt, Personality and
    Motives." *Journal of Applied Social Psychology* 24: 2132–2150.
Howell, S., and Marshall, B. 1998. "Crime and Trust in Local Govern-
    ment." *Urban Affairs Review* 33: 361–381.
Huddy, L., and Terkildsen, N. 1993. "Gender Stereotypes and the Per-
    ception of Male and Female Candidates." *American Journal of Po-
    litical Science* 37: 119–147.
Iyengar, S. and Kinder, D. 1987. *News That Matters*. Chicago: University
    of Chicago Press.
Jacobson, G., and Dimock, M. 1994. "Checking Out: The Effects of Bank
    Overdrafts on the 1992 House Elections." *American Journal of Po-
    litical Science* 38: 601–624.
Jamieson, K.H. 1992. *Dirty Politics*. New York: Oxford University Press.
Jamieson, K.H. 1995. *Beyond the Double Bind: Women and Leadership*. New
    York: Oxford University Press.
Jasperson, A., Shah, D., Watts, M., Faber, R., and Fan, D. 1998. "Framing
    and the Public Agenda: Media Effects on the Importance of the
    Federal Budget Deficit." *Political Communication* 15: 205–224.
Johnstone, J., Slawski, E., and Bowman, W. 1976. *The News People*.
    Urbana-Champaign: University of Illinois Press.
Just, M., Crigler, A., Alger, D., Cook, T., Kern, M., and West, D. 1996.
    *Crosstalk: Citizens, Candidates, and the Media in a Presidential Cam-
    paign*. Chicago: University of Chicago Press.
Just, M., Crigler, A., and Buhr, T. 1999. "Voice, Substance, and Cynicism
    in Presidential Campaign Media." *Political Communication* 16: 25–
    44.
Kahn, K. 1992. "Does Being Male Help?" *Journal of Politics* 54: 497–517.
Kahn, K., and Goldenberg, E. 1991. "Women Candidates in the News:
    An Examination of Gender Differences in U.S. Senate Campaign
    Coverage." *Public Opinion Quarterly* 55:180–199.
Kassin, S. 1997. "The Psychology of Confession Evidence." *American Psy-
    chologist* 52: 221–233
Kenney, K., and Simpson, C. 1993. "Was Coverage of the 1988 Presiden-
    tial Race by Washington's Two Major Dailies Biased?" *Journalism
    Quarterly* 70: 345–355.

Kerbel, M. 1995. *Remote and Controlled*. Boulder, CO: Westview Press.

Kernell, S. 1977. "Presidential Popularity and Negative Voting." *American Political Science Review* 71: 44–66.

King, E. 1995. "The Flawed Characters in the Campaign: Prestige Newspapers' Assessments of the 1992 Presidential Candidates' Integrity and Competence." *Journalism Quarterly* 72: 84–97.

King, E., and Schudson, M. 1995. "The Press and the Illusion of Public Opinion: The Strange Case of Ronald Reagan's 'Popularity.'" In *Public Opinion and the Communication of Consent*, T. Glasser and C. Salmon (eds.). New York: Guilford Press.

Klein, M., and Maccoby, N. 1954. "Newspaper Objectivity in the 1952 Campaign." *Journalism Quarterly* 31: 285–296.

Kobre, S. 1953. "How Florida Dailies Handled the 1952 Presidential Campaign." *Journalism Quarterly* 30: 163–169.

Koch, J. 1999. "Candidate Gender and Assessments of Senate Candidates." *Social Science Quarterly* 80, 84–96.

Kohut, A., and Toth, R. 1998. "The Central Conundrum: How Can People Like What They Distrust?" *Harvard International Journal of Press/Politics* 3: 110–117.

Kovach, B., and Rosenstiel, T. 1999. *Warp Speed*. New York: Century Foundation Press.

Kuklinski, J., and Sigelman, L. 1992. "When Objectivity is Not Objective: Network Television News Coverage of U.S. Senators and the 'Paradox of Objectivity.'" *Journal of Politics* 54: 810–833.

Kurtz, H. 1994. *Media Circus*. New York: Random House.

Kwak, N. 1999. "Revisiting the Knowledge Gap Hypothesis: Education, Motivation, and Media Use." *Communication Research* 26: 385–413.

Lasora, D. 1992. "How Media Affect Policy Makers: The Third Person Effect." In *Public Opinion, The Press, and Public Policy*, J.D. Kennamer (ed.). Westport, CT: Praeger.

Lau, R. 1985. "Two Explanations for Negativity Effects in Political Behavior." *American Journal of Political Science* 29: 119–138.

Levitt, S. 1997. "Using Electoral Cycles in Police Hiring to Estimate the Effect of Police on Crime." *American Economic Review* 87: 270–290.

Lichter, S.R., and Noyes, R. 1996. *Good Intentions Make Bad News*. Lanham, MD: Rowman and Littlefield.

Lichter, S.R., and Rothman, S. 1981. "Media and Business Elites." *Public Opinion* 5: 42–26, 59–60.

Lichter, S.R., Rothman, S., and Lichter, L. 1986. *The Media Elite*. Bethesda, MD: Adler and Adler.

Lipset, S., and Schneider, W. 1987. *The Confidence Gap*. Baltimore: Johns Hopkins University Press.

Lord, C., Ross, L., and Lepper, M. 1979. "Biased Assimilation and Attitude Polarization." *Journal of Personality and Social Psychology* 37: 2098–2109.

Lowden, N., Andersen, P., and Dozier, D. 1994. "Media Use in the Primary Election: a Secondary Medium Model." *Communication Research* 21: 293–304.

Lowry, D. 1974. "Measures of Network News Bias in the 1972 Presidential Campaign." *Journal of Broadcasting* 18: 387–402.

Lowry, D., and Shidler, J. 1995. "The Sound Bites, the Biters, and the Bitten: An Analysis of Network TV News Bias in Campaign '92." *Journalism and Mass Communication Quarterly* 72: 33–44.

Malaney, G., and Buss, T. 1979. "AP Wire Reports vs. CBS TV News Coverage of a Presidential Campaign." *Journalism Quarterly* 56: 602–610.

Mann, L. 1974. "Counting the Crowd: Effects of Editorial Policy on Estimates." *Journalism Quarterly* 51: 278–285.

Mantler, G., and Whiteman, D. 1995. "Attention to Candidates and Issues in Newspaper Coverage of 1992 Presidential Campaign." *Newspaper Research Journal* 16: 14–28.

Martindale, C. and Dunlap, L.R. 1997. "The African Americans." In *U.S. News Coverage of Racial Minorities*, B. Keever, C. Martindale, and M. Weston (eds.). Westport, CT: Greenwood Press.

Maurer, P. 1999. "Media Feeding Frenzies: Press Behavior During Two Clinton Scandals." *Presidential Studies Quarterly* 29: 65–79.

McCarthy, J., McPhail, C., and Smith, J. 1996. "Images of Protest: Dimensions of Selection Bias in Media Coverage of Washington Demonstrations, 1982 and 1991." *American Sociological Review* 61: 478–499.

McCord, L., and Weaver, J. 1996. "Biased Coverage of the 1992 U.S. Presidential Campaign in *Time, Newsweek*, and *U.S. News and World Report.*" Presented to the Annual Meeting of the Speech Communication Association, San Diego, CA.

Meadow, R. 1973. "Cross-media Comparison of Coverage of the 1972 Presidential Campaign." *Journalism Quarterly* 50: 482–488.

Meffert, M. 2000. "Political Information Flow in Context: Media Effects, Personal Networks, and the Mass Public." Ph.D. dissertation, State University of New York, Stony Brook.

Mendelsohn, M. 1998. "The Construction of Electoral Mandates: Media Coverage of Election Results in Canada." *Political Communication* 15: 239–253.

Miller, A., Goldenberg, E., and Erbring, L. 1979. "Type-Set Politics: The Impact of Newspapers on Public Confidence." *American Political Science Review* 73: 67–84.

Mills, K. 1997. "What Difference do Women Journalists Make?" In

Women, Media, and Politics, P. Norris (ed.). New York: Oxford University Press.

Millspaugh, M. 1949. "Baltimore Newspapers and the Presidential Election." *Public Opinion Quarterly* 13: 122–123.

Moriarty, S., and Garramone, G. 1986. "A Study of Newsmagazine Photographs of the 1984 Presidential Campaign." *Journalism Quarterly* 63: 728–734.

Moriarty, S., and Popovich, M. 1991. "Newsmagazine Visuals and the 1988 Presidential Election." *Journalism Quarterly* 68: 371–380.

Moy, P., Pfau, M., and Kahlor, L. 1999. "Media Use and Public Confidence in Democratic Institutions." *Journal of Broadcasting and Electronic Media* 43: 137–158.

Mullen, B., Futrell, D., Stairs, D., Tice, D., Baumeister, R., Dawson, K., Riordan, C., Radloff, C., Goethals, G., Kennedy, J., and Rosenfeld, P. 1986. "Newscasters' Facial Expressions and Voting Behavior of Viewers: Can a Smile Elect a President?" *Journal of Personality and Social Psychology* 51: 291–295.

Murphy, J. 1998. "An Analysis of Political Bias in Evening Network News During the 1996 Presidential Campaign." Ph.D. dissertation, University of Oklahoma.

Mutz, D., and Soss, J. 1997. "Reading Public Opinion: The Influence of News Coverage on Perceptions of Public Sentiment." *Public Opinion Quarterly* 61: 431–451.

Niven, D., and Zilber, J. 2001. "How Does She Have Time for Kids and Congress? Views on Gender and Media Coverage from House Offices." *Women and Politics* 23: 147–165.

Nollet, M. 1968. "The *Boston Globe* in Four Presidential Elections." *Journalism Quarterly* 45: 531–532.

Olasky, M. 1988a. *The Press and Abortion, 1838–1988*. Hillsdale, NJ: Lawrence Erlbaum Associates.

Olasky, M. 1988b. *Prodigal Press: The Anti-Christian Bias of the American News Media*. Westchester, IL: Crossway Books.

Ornstein, N., and Robinson, M. 1990. "Why Press Credibility is Going Down (And What to Do About It)." *Washington Journalism Review* 12: 34–37.

Page, B., and Shapiro, R. 1992. *The Rational Public*. Chicago: University of Chicago Press.

Patterson, T. 1980. *The Mass Media Election*. Westport, CT: Praeger.

Patterson, T. 1994. *Out of Order*. New York: Vintage.

Patterson, T., and Donsbach, W. 1996. "News Decisions: Journalists as Partisan Actors." *Political Communication* 13: 455–468.

Patterson, T., and McClure, R. 1976. *The Unseeing Eye*. New York: Putnam.

Payne, J.G. 1988. "Shaping the Race Issue: A Special Kind of Journalism." *Political Communication and Persuasion* 5: 145–160.

Peters, J., and Welch, S. 1980. "The Effects of Charges of Corruption on Voting Behavior in Congressional Elections." *American Political Science Review* 74: 697–708.

Pew Center. 1998. "Internet News Takes Off: Event-Driven News Audiences." Report of the Pew Research Center for the People and the Press, Washington, DC.

Pinkleton, B., Austin, E., and Fortman, K. 1998. "Relationships of Media Use and Political Disaffection to Political Efficacy and Voting Behavior." *Journal of Broadcasting and Electronic Media* 42: 34–49.

Popovich, M., Moriarty, S., and Pitts, B. 1993. "News Magazine Coverage of the 1988 Presidential Campaign." *Mass Communication Review* 20: 99–110.

Povich, E. 1996. *Partners and Adversaries.* Washington, DC: The Freedom Forum.

Price, G. 1954. "A Method for Analyzing Newspaper Campaign Coverage." *Journalism Quarterly* 31: 447–458.

Reeves, K. 1997. *Voting Hopes or Fears? White Voters, Black Candidates and Racial Politics in America.* New York: Oxford University Press.

Reeves, R. 1997. "The Question of Media Bias." In *Do the Media Govern?,* S. Iyengar and R. Reeves (eds.). Thousand Oaks, CA: Sage.

Repass, D., and Chaffee, S. 1968. "Administration vs. Campaign Coverage of Two Presidents in Eight Partisan Dailies." *Journalism Quarterly* 45: 528–531.

Rimmer, T., and Weaver, D. 1987. "Different Questions, Different Answers." *Journalism Quarterly* 64: 28–44.

Rivers, W. 1962. "The Correspondents After 25 Years." *Columbia Journalism Review* 1: 5.

Robinson, John, and Michael Levy. 1985. *The Main Source: Learning from Televison News.* Beverly Hills: Sage.

Robinson, M. 1974. "The Impact of Televised Watergate Hearings." *Journal of Communication* 24: 17–30.

Robinson, M. 1976. "Public Affairs Television and the Growth of Political Malaise." *American Political Science Review* 70: 409–432.

Robinson, M. 1983. "Just How Liberal is the News? 1980 Revisited." *Public Opinion* 7: 55–60.

Robinson, M. 1985. "The Media in Campaign '84." *Public Opinion* 9: 55–60.

Robinson, M. 1986. "Pressing Opinion." *Public Opinion* 9: 56–59.

Robinson, M., and Kohut, A. 1988. "Believability and the Press." *Public Opinion Quarterly* 52: 174–189.

Robinson, M., and Sheehan, M. 1983. *Over the Wire and On TV.* New York: Russell Sage Foundation.

Roshcoe, B. 1975. *Newsmaking*. Chicago: University of Chicago Press.

Rosten, L. 1937. *The Washington Correspondents*. New York: Harcourt, Brace.

Rothman, S., and Lichter, S.R. 1987. "Elite Ideology and Risk Perception in Nuclear Energy Policy." *American Political Science Review* 81(2): 383–404.

Rozell, M. 1994. "Press Coverage of Congress." In *Congress, the Press, and the Public*, T. Mann and N. Ornstein (eds.). Washington, DC: American Enterprise Institute.

Ryan, C. 1991. *Prime Time Activism*. Boston: South End Press.

Sabato, L. 1991. *Feeding Frenzy*. New York: Free Press.

Salwen, M. 1998. "Perceptions of Media Influence and Support for Censorship: The Third-Person Effect in the 1996 Presidential Election." *Communication Research* 25: 259–285.

Schneider, W., and Lewis, I. 1985. "Views on the News." *Public Opinion* 8: 6–11, 58–59.

Sears, D. 1986. "College Sophomores in the Laboratory: Influences of a Narrow Data Base on Social Psychology's View of Human Nature." *Journal of Personality and Social Psychology* 51: 515–530.

Shaw, D., and Sparrow, B. 1999. "From the Inner Ring Out: News Congruence, Cue-Taking, and Campaign Coverage." *Political Research Quarterly* 52: 323–351.

Shoemaker, P., and Reese, S. 1991. *Mediating the Message: Theories of Influences on Mass Media Content*. New York: Longman.

Short, R. 2000. "Modern Racism and the Linguistic Intergroup Bias: An Empirical Investigation." Ph.D. dissertation, Claremont Graduate University, California.

Sigal, L. 1973. *Reporters and Officials*. Lexington, MA: Heath.

Simon, R. 1998. *Show Time: The American Political Circus and the Race for the White House*. New York: Times Books.

Smoller, F. 1990. *The Six O'Clock Presidency: A Theory of Presidential Press Relations in the Age of Television*. Westport, CT: Praeger.

Solomon, N. 1999. *The Habits of Highly Deceptive Media: Decoding Spin and Lies in Mainstream News*. Monroe, ME: Common Courage Press.

Staten, C., and Sloss, G. 1993. "The Media and Politics: A Content Analysis of the *Louisville Courier-Journal* During the 1992 Presidential Election." *Journal of Political Science* 21: 90–98.

Stempel, G. 1961. "The Prestige Press Covers the 1960 Presidential Campaign." *Journalism Quarterly* 38: 157–163.

Stempel, G. 1965. "The Prestige Press in Two Presidential Elections." *Journalism Quarterly* 42: 15–21.

Stempel, G. 1969. "The Prestige Press Meets the Third-Party Challenge." *Journalism Quarterly* 46: 699–706.

Stempel, G. 1991. "Media Coverage of Presidential Campaigns as a Political Issue." In *The Media in the 1984 and 1988 Presidential Campaigns*, G. Stempel and J. Windhauser (eds.). Westport, CT: Greenwood.

Stempel, G., and Windhauser, J. 1984. "The Prestige Press Revisited: The 1980 Presidential Campaign." *Journalism Quarterly* 61: 49–55.

Stempel, G., and Windhauser, J. 1989. "Coverage by the Prestige Press of the 1988 Presidential Campaign." *Journalism Quarterly* 66: 894–896, 919.

Stempel, G., and Windhauser, J. 1991. "Newspaper Coverage of the 1984 and 1988 Campaigns." In *The Media in the 1984 and 1988 Presidential Campaigns*, G. Stempel and J. Windhauser (eds.). Westport, CT: Greenwood.

Stevenson, R., Eisinger, R., Feinberg, B, and Kotak, A. 1973. "Untwisting *The News Twisters*: A Replication of Efron's Study." *Journalism Quarterly* 50: 211–219.

Stevenson, R., and Greene, M. 1980. "A Reconsideration of Bias in the News." *Journalism Quarterly* 62: 266–271.

Stewart, C. 1994. "Let's Go Fly a Kite: Correlates of Involvement in the House Bank Scandal." *Legislative Studies Quarterly* 19: 521–536.

Stovall, J. 1985. "The Third Party Challenge of 1980: News Coverage of Presidential Candidates." *Journalism Quarterly* 62: 266–271.

Stovall, J. 1988. "Coverage of the 1984 Presidential Campaign." *Journalism Quarterly* 65: 443–449, 484.

Terkildsen, N., and Damore, D. 1999. "The Dynamics of Racialized Media Coverage in Congressional Elections." *Journal of Politics* 61: 680–699.

Tiedge, J., Silverblatt, A., Havice, M., and Rosenfield, R. 1991. "Discrepancy Between Perceived First-Person and Perceived Third-Person Mass Media Effects." *Journalism Quarterly* 68: 141–154.

Tuchman, G. 1978. *Making News: A Study in the Construction of Reality*. New York: Free Press.

Vallone, R., Ross, L., and Lepper, M. 1985. "The Hostile Media Phenomenon: Biased Perception and Perceptions of Media Bias in Coverage of the Beirut Massacre." *Journal of Personality and Social Psychology* 49: 577–585.

Waldman, P., and Devitt, J. 1998. "Newspaper Photographs and the 1996 Presidential Election: The Question of Bias." *Journalism and Mass Communication Quarterly* 75: 302–311.

Watts, M., Domke, D., Shah, D., and Fan, D. 1999. "Elite Cues and Media Bias in Presidential Campaigns." *Communication Research* 26(2): 144–175.

Weaver, D. 1997. "Women as Journalists." In *Women, Media, and Politics*, P. Norris (ed.). New York: Oxford University Press.

Welch, S., and Hibbing, J. 1997. "The Effects of Charges of Corruption on Voting Behavior in Congressional Elections, 1982–1990." *Journal of Politics* 59: 226–239.

Westley, B., Higbie, C., Burke, T., Lippert, D., Maurer, L., and Stone, V. 1963. "The Newsmagazines and the 1960 Conventions." *Journalism Quarterly* 40: 525–531, 647.

Wilhoit, G., Weaver, D., and Gray, R. 1986. *The American Journalist*. Bloomington: Indiana University Press.

Wilkins, K. 2000. "The Role of Media in Public Disengagement from Political Life." *Journal of Broadcasting and Electronic Media* 44: 569–580.

Windhauser, J., and Evarts, D. 1991. "Watching the Campaigns on Network Television." In *The Media in the 1984 and 1988 Presidential Campaigns*, G. Stempel and J. Windhauser (eds.). Westport, CT: Greenwood.

Witt, L., Paget, K., and Matthews, G. 1995. *Running as a Woman: Gender and Power in American Politics*. New York: Free Press.

Woodard, J. 1994. "Coverage of Elections on Evening Television News Shows: 1972–1992." In *Presidential Campaigns and American Self Images*, A. Miller and B. Gronbeck (eds.). Boulder, CO: Westview.

Zaller, J., and Chiu, D. 1996. "Government's Little Helper: U.S. Press Coverage of Foreign Policy Crises, 1945–1991." *Political Communication* 13: 385–405.

Zilber, J., and Niven, D. 2000. *Racialized Coverage of Congress: The News in Black and White*. Westport, CT: Praeger.

Zukin, C. 1981. "Mass Communication and Public Opinion." In *Handbook of Political Communication*, D. Nimmo and K. Sanders (eds.). Beverly Hills, CA: Sage.

Index

About the Author

DAVID NIVEN is an Associate Professor in the Department of Political Science at Florida Atlantic University. He is the author of *The Missing Majority: The Recruitment of Women as State Legislative Candidates* (Praeger, 1998) and co-author of *Racialized Coverage of Congress: The News in Black and White* (Praeger, 2000).